COMMUNITY ACTION

COMMUNITY

Henri Lamoureux · Robert Mayer · Jean Panet-Raymond

ACTion

BLACK
ROSE
BOOKS

Montréal - New York

Black Rose Books No. Q124

Hardcover ISBN: 0-921689-21-7
Paperback ISBN: 0-921689-20-9

Canadian Cataloguing in Publication Data

Lamoureux, Henri, 1942-
Community action

Translation of: L'intervention communautaire.
Bibliography: p.
ISBN: 0-921689-21-7 (bound)
ISBN: 0-921689-20-9 (pbk.)
1. Community organization--Quebec (Province) 2. Social
participation--Quebec (Province) 3. Social action--Quebec
(Province). 4. Social service--Quebec (Province)--Citizen
participation.
I. Mayer, Robert, 1943- II. Panet-Raymond, Jean III. Title.

HN49.C6L3413 1988   361.8'09714 C88-090105-5

Cover design: Richard Parent

BLACK ROSE BOOKS

3981 boul. St-Laurent, #444
Montréal, Québec H2W 1Y5
Canada

340 Nagel Drive
Cheektowaga, N.Y. 14225
USA

Printed and Bound in Québec, Canada

TABLE OF CONTENTS

PREFACE

This important book fills a gap in the literature on community action in Canada. It is based on two decades of organizing experience from the period of the Quiet Revolution to the Eighties. For English-language readers, it offers a glimpse of the political vitality of community groups in Québec as well as the diversity of community initiatives.

The book can be read at two levels: as a series of case studies and as an organizing manual.

As a series of case studies, it is part of a small but growing literature in Québec and Canada that illustrates the significance of community in the life of a people. Much of the literature focuses on the relationship of community work, the labour movement, and political action. And this book is no exception. Whether it is Québec neighbours fighting city hall, welfare recipients claiming fair treatment, women demanding employment equity, environmentalists pushing for pollution controls, or peace groups organizing for disarmament, the message is the same. People want a democratic society in which they have control over the economic and political decisions that affect their everyday lives.

The authors also illustrate another important point. Community action in Québec no longer represents a form of passive populism through which partisan political demands are channeled, or a traditional patron-client relationship in which private interests respond paternalistically to those in need. Instead, it serves to highlight the contradictions of the welfare state, particularly those contradictions that lead to the subordination and dependence of the very people whom the State was intended to assist.

As an organizing manual, the book provides many practical examples of strategy and tactics. While the authors do not ignore the limitations of community action, they nevertheless stress the potential of community organization as a key element in political education. For that reason, they feel that community activists and community workers cannot afford to ignore the need for some professional expertise. They are particularly good in examining issues like ideology, research, community profiles, mobilization, struggle, and group process.

The authors attach considerable importance to a knowledge of the basic skills of organizing as an efficient and effective means of assuring the development of an active participatory democracy. They do not mystify or professionalize the community action process. What they set out to do, and achieve with considerable success, is provide a guide for individuals engaged in community organization who need some seasoned advice. One reason why they succeed is the writing style of the manual, which is intentionally popular. Happily, it is free of technical jargon. The English translation should be in as much demand as its French counterpart.

Glenn Drover
School of Social Work
University of British Columbia
Vancouver

TRANSLATORS' PREFACE

In translating this book, two terms gave us particular difficulty: *animation sociale* and *populaire*. *Animation sociale* refers to the particular style of community work related to the citizens' groups prevalent in Québec in the late Sixties and early Seventies. In Chapter Two, the authors discuss this approach and its underlying ideology. We decided to translate it as "social animation" to distinguish it as a specific form of community organizing practice that, while it undoubtedly existed elsewhere in North America, does not seem to have been designated by any particular English term.

As for *populaire* (in the sense of "of or for the people"), we considered "people's," "mass," "grass-roots," "citizens'," and "working-class," all of which are frequently used to translate *populaire*. However, none of these words quite did the job in certain contexts. For example, the authors distinguish between "citizens' groups," "community groups," and "popular groups." We finally opted to use terms such as "popular groups," "popular organizations," "the popular movement," and "popular education." This use of "popular" seems to be more and more prevalent in North America, perhaps due to Latin American influences. An example is the "Popular Summit" that took place in Toronto while the leaders of the big seven industrialized nations held their economic summit. The term *populaire* refers to a specific way of seeing the world, and a specific approach to organizing, and we felt "popular" was the best choice to render that perspective in English.

FOREWORD TO THE
ENGLISH-LANGUAGE EDITION

This English-language edition of *Community Action: Organizing for Social Change* is slightly different from the original French edition. Since the book is based on the experience of community organizing in Québec, we have made a few changes to help readers understand the Québec context.

We feel that the community groups and public institutions involved in health and social services in Québec illustrate Québec's uniqueness. They have developed in response to the needs of the people of Québec, as an integral part of a true nation that is different both from the rest of Canada and from other English-speaking countries, and that values that difference.

We see our experience in community organization as part of the unique process of development of Québec society. Our difference, however, has not isolated us from the trends that have affected Western society; on the contrary, our development has been enriched by contact with British, American, Canadian, and Latin American experience in community organization. We hope this book will contribute to a better understanding of Québec's unique development and particularly of our special and original responses to problems that are faced everywhere.

INTRODUCTION

For many people, community organizing has become a job, with all the rules and limitations that any job entails. For most, however, community organizing is a way of taking part in building a better society for everyone. Whether paid or not, the women and men involved in organizing their communities share a common endeavour: to ensure an equitable distribution of knowledge, wealth, and power, and, since our social structure is the cause of many injustices, to change that system, or at least to correct some of its imbalances. It follows, then, that many of the activities related to community organizing involve conflict.

The above statement will help identify where the authors stand. We are speaking from our experience in the field, and the field is not neutral. It is an arena in which social agents with antagonistic interests confront each other. Our practice has made us aware of the inequalities that exist between women and men, among social classes, between the haves and the have-nots. We recognize that real power rests in the hands of a tiny minority. Although knowledge belongs to everyone, life experience is looked down on and is rarely validated by diplomas. A large part of our collective wealth has been appropriated by smaller and smaller numbers of individuals. We believe that it is necessary to radically change this state of affairs.

There is a variety of conceptions of what community organization should be. We have been influenced by several schools. We cannot ignore the important theoretical contributions of Ross, Piven and

Cloward, Alinsky, and others included in our bibliography. The work of Barclay in England has also had a major impact on the development of community work in State social service institutions in Québec. In addition, Latin Americans such as Freire have a significant Québec following. We should also acknowledge the important contribution of our colleagues in Québec to the understanding of community organizing.

In our view, community organization is a form of *praxis*. While it involves individuals joining together to provide services and educational activities for themselves, these activities are designed not only to make them better able to "take responsibility for themselves,"[1] but also, and much more importantly, to win them individual and collective power. In this sense, community organizing is also a form of political organizing, but one that focuses on change and that is governed by different rules than those governing partisan politics.

The goals of community organizing are broader and more meaningful than, for example, the "community approach" currently favoured by the Québec government. That concept, in our view, refers more to a strategy of transferring State responsibilities to individuals and communities, who are asked, largely on a volunteer basis, to fill the gaps in services left by the withdrawal of the State. It definitely does *not* mean the involvement of communities in a democratic process that will enable them to exercise real power over their social environment. Community organizing cannot be reduced to such an approach or allow itself to be the extension of a strategy of State disengagement from social services.

This manual is intended for organizers involved in popular groups, the women's movement, peace and disarmament groups, environmentalist groups, and groups exploring new forms of economic development. There are more than four thousand such groups in Québec, according to an 1987 estimate, and they represent an important part of the forces for progress. We hope this book will also be a useful tool for students, not only those studying social work but also students in other disciplines related to community organizing. We also hope it will interest employees of the State, particularly in the institutions of the ministry of health and social services.

The examples cited in this book are in large part taken from the personal experience of the authors, who have been active in the popular movement for twenty years and who also teach at the university level. In spite of the wealth of experience of the popular movement in Québec, it has been the subject of very little formal analysis. Although this situation has improved somewhat in the last few years, the achievements of the groups involved in community organizing have been passed on essentially through the oral tradition, and each new generation of organizers has had to cover the same ground and make the same mistakes. It is possible to follow the development of community organizing in Québec, however, by reading old newspaper articles or by studying the self-evaluations done by organizations. Since the beginning of the Eighties, some groups have published books about their experience. These include the *Centre des Femmes des Cantons* (Eastern Townships Women's Centre) in Cowansville and the Citizens' Committee of Valleyfield, which has been fighting to improve the quality of drinking water in that town. They have provided extremely useful reference books and we hope that more groups will follow their example and describe their own experiences.

Community organizing has its own rules, and these rules constitute the basic content of our book. We have tried to produce a practical guide, one that, while it cannot provide "recipes," covers the essentials of community organizing. We hope we have been successful.

I

COMMUNITY ORGANIZING:
People, Places, Issues

It is not a good idea to confine the practice of community organization within a rigid definition. This would be too restrictive and might lead some people to recognize only those strategies of community organization that fit the definition. We will, however, suggest certain guidelines for identifying approaches that draw on the principles of community organizing.

First of all, community organizing can be carried out only by bringing together people who, directly or indirectly, have common interests. It is democratic, in the sense that the action has a democratic objective such as the affirmation or exercise of a right. The democratic aspect of community organizing should be reflected in the internal functioning of the group, in terms of both decision-making structures and the emphasis placed on the participation of all members. Community organization is also an educational process that validates people's existing knowledge and skills and enables them to acquire new ones. Finally, any strategy of community organization should aim to bring about change, to reduce or eliminate exploitation, oppression, and alienation. From this perspective, it is not just another "approach," a new, more economical or efficient way of "managing" social problems. Nor is it diametrically opposed to individual approaches, since in many groups organizers can also be involved in working individually with members who participate in group activities.

Saul Alinsky best summarized the goal of community organization in his well-known book *Rules for Radicals:* "There can be no darker or more devastating tragedy than the death of man's faith in himself and in his power to direct his future." [2] We would add that what is true for an individual is also true for a people, a collectivity, or a community. Community organization is an expression of people's faith in their own ability to defend their individual and collective rights and interests. At the same time, it brings out the contradictions inherent in the practice of democracy in a society such as ours.

In the following pages, we will deal with various aspects of community organization. We will look at its history in Québec, in particular at the reaction of the State to the use of this strategy. This historical overview will also illustrate the importance of community organizing efforts in the political development of modern Québec. We will discuss the women and men involved in community organization and the various settings in which they work. We will also look at some of the factors that give the practice of community organization in Québec its unique character.

One

A BRIEF HISTORY

Through the ages, human beings have sought to control their own destiny. The development of democracy is an expression of this fundamental human striving, and community organizing has a key role in the development of democracy. It expresses the pressing need we feel to be actors, creators of our own social life and of the structures that determine the quality of life. It is the affirmation of fundamental rights without which democracy is nothing but an illusion. It is also the acceptance of personal responsibility for solving the community's problems. Finally, it is an act of opposition, a refusal to accept the authoritarianism of the decision-making mechanisms of our society and the bureaucratic management of resources by the State.

The people of Québec have a wealth of experience in the area of community organization. For the purposes of this book, we will confine ourselves to that of the last thirty years.

The Emergence of Modern Québec

The development of community organization in Québec reflects the development of our society as a whole. The rapid transformation of Québec into an advanced industrial society had a significant effect on working people, both urban and rural. Structural changes in the industrial and agricultural sectors of the Québec economy since the end of World War II necessitated a rapid reorganization of education, health, and social services, a reassessment of economic planning, and massive investments in the construction of access routes to resources and markets. As a result, there was a substantial increase in State involvement in the economy and a redeployment of resources towards those areas.

This modernization had important consequences for the people and communities involved. A large part of the housing stock was threatened with demolition to make way for highways, luxury apartment towers, office buildings, and shops. Citizens' groups, in turn, demanded respect for the integrity of working-class neighbourhoods and residential areas in general, renovation of housing, rent control, and other measures favouring the "right to housing." (It should be noted that in 1987, as the activities of FRAPRU[3] and the Overdale Tenants' Association[4] show, the issue of housing still mobilizes large numbers of people. We will return later to these examples.)

Health became a major issue when reports were made public showing that a large segment of the population did not have access to adequate services, or that the services available were so expensive that people were forced to go into debt to pay for them. Consumer organizations such as the ACEFs[5] were formed to fight against financial sharks of all shapes and sizes.

Encouraged by increasingly powerful union organizations, the struggle for improved living conditions was for a time seen as a "second front," of equal importance to the struggle for improved working conditions. In addition, the democratization of access to education led to the emergence of a new salaried petty bourgeoisie, a segment of which supported working-class causes, and to the creation of community development groups. Finally, the Québec struggle for sovereignty, together with a growing interest in socialism, stimulated the development of a variety of strategies of community organization.

The State was at first relatively receptive to the new desire for participation. It encouraged this trend through some funding of research and social animation. The State even took some initiatives of its own, such as the creation of the BAEQ,[6] which, it would later become apparent, was nothing more than a way of getting the population of the

Lower St-Lawrence region to accept government development plans involving the displacement of large numbers of people and the closing of many villages.

Reports by several commissions of inquiry led to the adoption of a whole series of laws aimed at rationalizing public administration and establishing new structures in the areas of health, social services, education, justice, and income security. These laws sometimes stimulated the creation of new groups. For example, ADDS[7] discovered that the "rights" granted by welfare law reform were not always applied with due speed and generosity. Welfare rights advocates were trained in order to ensure that the rights of welfare recipients were not infringed upon by the abusive regulations and the nit-picking administration of a law that decreed the living conditions of nearly 650,000 people.

Food coops[8] were set up in response to increases in the cost of living. The precarious situation of the aged prompted action to ensure that they would receive at least minimal services so that they could continue living at home. Many organizations, such as ASTA and Place Vermeil,[9] which were created in the early Seventies, continue to be much appreciated by retired people. In the early Seventies a great many groups were set up to deal with issues concerning quality of life at the neighbourhood level. They were run by representatives of the local population, and they demanded greater participation in the structures of democracy and more social investment in needy communities.

Years of Turmoil, Consolidation, and Development

The beginning of the Seventies marked an abrupt turn in Québec politics. The Parti québécois was increasing its membership and its share of the vote. The union movement was taking ever more progressive positions, including calling for the creation of a second front on living conditions. As part of this current, a coalition of popular groups and trade unionists in Montréal founded FRAP,[10] a socialist party that planned to take on the entrenched city administration of Mayor Jean Drapeau. Some Québec independence groups, meanwhile, stepped up their use of high-profile tactics such as mass demonstrations and bombings. (The situation culminated in the kidnappings of the minister of labour and a British diplomat in October 1970.) The political excitement was a sign of the vitality not only of the unions but also of the increasingly dynamic popular movement. The declaration of the War Measures Act in October 1970[11] brought these developments to a brutal halt.

In spite of this painful beginning, progress in the Seventies continued at breakneck speed. It was a decisive period in the development of community organization. At the start of the decade Québec had enough human and financial resources to initiate a rapid and extensive process of reform, largely in response to demands being expressed, in increasingly disruptive ways, by the popular movement. The first CLSCs[12] and the first legal aid offices were created. The government also announced a whole series of legislative reforms involving consumer protection, tenants' rights, and improved working conditions for minimum-wage workers. In some cases these reforms led to the demise of grass-roots organizations. Some were simply absorbed into the new State institutions, while others found themselves unable to compete. With some fulfilment of their short-term demands, the popular groups shifted focus. While continuing to demand that the State satisfy the most pressing social needs, many groups were becoming increasingly aware of issues related to the vitality of democracy in our society.

The Seventies marked a breakdown in the alliances formed in the Sixties during the Quiet Revolution.[13] This breakdown prompted the development of new social movements and the unification of a large segment of the progressive forces in Québec around the social programme promoted by the Parti québécois.

The first half of the decade saw the consolidation of various organizations involved in community development. ACEFs became more and more numerous, dozens of consumer associations sprang up, food coops expanded, ADDS groups mushroomed and organized significant battles, and the popular education movement experienced spectacular growth. New groups emerged: community daycare centres, worker cooperatives, and community media. Political theatre groups and progressive filmmakers, writers, and musicians appeared on the cultural front. Associations were formed to defend the rights of retired people, the handicapped, and injured workers. The high level of illiteracy prompted the organization of literacy campaigns by grass-roots groups. At major demonstrations, such as those held on May 1,[14] the banners of popular groups fluttered in the wind alongside those of the unions.

In 1976, after losing two previous elections, the Parti québécois was swept to power in an atmosphere of euphoria. For a while, popular organizations and unions had the feeling that their interests were finally represented in the National Assembly. This impression was based on the fact that many of the newly elected members came from unions and popular groups. During the same period, the Montréal Citizens' Movement succeeded in getting a few city councillors elected, some of whom were also from the union and popular movements. The honeymoon with the Parti québécois lasted two years. With the first signs of a major recession, the party's "pro-worker bias" began to be less and less in evidence.

The Seventies also saw the emergence, and the eventual break-up, of several political organizations claiming to be Marxist-Leninist. These included In Struggle and the Communist League (Marxist-Leninist), which later became the Workers' Communist Party. For many social activists, these organizations provided an opportunity to be in the forefront of partisan politics without having to compromise their basic values or their commitment to unions or popular groups. There was criticism, within popular groups, of the activities of these organizations and of their dogmatism. The tactic of packing groups, often used by Marxist-Leninist activists, has been frequently denounced, in our view quite rightly; such practices led to a degree of demobilization in popular groups. We believe, though, that too much has been blamed on the Marxist-Leninists; their activities, however dubious, were not the only cause of demobilization.

The beginning of the Eighties was, like the end of the Sixties, a time of questioning. Disappointed with politics, and having become cautious with age and the desire for security, many Sixties and Seventies activists abandoned community organizing for other activities. In spite of the recession, however, which hit ordinary working people particularly hard, and in spite of the sadness over the defeat of the referendum on Québec sovereignty, many social activists were still involved in community groups. The popular movement continued to make progress and to expand into new areas. An example is the women's movement.

Years of Renewal

The feminist movement got its start in the early Seventies with the Front de libération des femmes (Women's Liberation Front) and publications such as *Québécoises debouttes!* (Québec Women, Rise Up!). Since the beginning of the Eighties, the Québec feminist movement has undergone a spectacular expansion, making it one of the most dynamic in the world. It has drained some energy from the popular movement, but it has also created new energies, initiating important struggles on many fronts — job equity, pornography, sexism, health care that respects women, free and accessible abortion services, recognition of the economic value of housework, and the struggle against rape and violence against women.

The feminist movement brought out the importance of women's involvement in community development. Its criticisms also stimulated a significant reconsideration of women's role in union and popular organizations. Raising fundamental ethical questions, the feminist movement has today become the only popular forum for the discussion of important social issues such as the revolution in reproductive technology. By the mid-Eighties the Québec women's movement consisted of nearly fifteen hundred groups organized in fifteen federations, such as the Associations féminines d'Education et d'Action sociale (AFEAS),[15] the Regroupement des Centres de Femmes (Federation of Women's Centres),[16] and the Regroupement des Maisons d'Hébergement (Federation of Women's Shelters).[17] It represents a major force in community organization.

There has been expansion on other fronts as well, in spite of the economic recession and the rise of conservatism. The ecology and peace movements have done important educational work that has begun to bring concrete results. Young people have managed to establish a network of resources to try to counter a major deterioration in their living conditions. Organizations such as the AQDR,[18] representing retired people, have succeeded, through a remarkable mobilization effort, in stopping federal cuts in old-age pensions.

The recession and neo-conservative remedies for it have resulted in high levels of unemployment. This situation has led to defensive struggles and the creation of a network of grass-roots services to aid and inform the unemployed. It has also stimulated the formation of groups active in the economic sphere. Production cooperatives have grown in number and have formed a Québec-wide federation. In several regions of Québec and in some Montréal neighbourhoods, economic development corporations have been set up to promote job creation. Their orientation is not always compatible with the ethics of community organizing and they have met with mixed results. In some cases several groups have joined together on a regional basis to maximize their impact. Two examples of these new economic development projects are the Corporation du Développement communautaire des Bois-Francs in Victoriaville and the Programme économique de Pointe St-Charles (PEP). The expansion of community organizing into the economic sphere is one of the most significant innovations of the late Eighties. It remains to be seen how these initiatives will develop and what links the "economic" groups will be able to establish with groups that have a more "social" orientation.

In political terms, the Eighties, as we have seen, began with the referendum defeat. The Parti québécois was re-elected in 1981 and immediately faced major conflicts with the union movement, particularly the public sector unions. Plagued with problems, the P.Q. government was replaced by the Liberals in 1985. In Ottawa, the Conservatives came to power in 1984. In Montréal, the Montréal Citizens' Movement won a decisive victory in the 1986 municipal elections, virtually wiping out the party that had annihilated the Front d'action politique (FRAP) in 1970.

People active in community groups and unions are now showing a great deal of caution with regard to partisan politics. The election of the Montréal Citizens' Movement does not appear to have changed this attitude, since all parties that claim to be social democratic seem to dilute their programmes as soon as they get close to power.

This leads us to two conclusions. First, it is clear that partisan politics can no longer be seen as the only forum for political action. Groups are discovering, for example, that a well-orchestrated lobby can be more effective than relying on the campaign promises of a politician whose power is very limited, given the political ethic of favouring the interests of the party over those of the voters. Secondly, the loss of confidence in partisan political activity could lead groups to set up broader structures of representation. This would put them on a more equal footing with employers' groups, which are becoming more and more powerful, unions, which are leaning towards an increasingly overt corporatism, and professional corporations, which are becoming more aggressive. The popular movement could constitute a fourth power in Québec society, one that represents the interests of welfare recipients and the working poor.

The capacity to move on to a new stage of organization in which groups involved in community organization could affirm their collective identity may well be the key development of the next decade.

NOTES

1. Translators' note: "Taking responsibility" has become a catchphrase in the State health and social service establishments.

2. New York: Random House, 1971, p. xxvi.

3. The Front d'action populaire et de réaménagement urbain (Front for Popular Action on Urban Planning) is a provincial organization that carries out research and action to promote the interests of working-class people in the area of housing and urban planning.

4. The Overdale Tenants' Association was formed in Montréal in response to a development project that would displace these tenants from their homes. The association undertook a struggle against the developers and against a city administration that was generally considered sympathetic to people in working-class neighbourhoods.

5. The Associations coopératives d'économie familiale (Cooperative Family Budget Associations) were born in the mid-Sixties as an extension of the work of the Confédération des syndicats nationaux (CSN) - Confederation of National Trade Unions (CNTU) - into the area of consumerism. They are based on the work of Ralph Nader but have since developed their own approaches.

6. The Bureau d'aménagement de l'est du Québec (Eastern Québec Planning and Development Office) involved a large-scale social animation programme with the population of the Gaspé Peninsula and the Lower St. Lawrence region in the Sixties. When people realized that this was intended to manipulate them rather than to involve them in planning and development for their region, they banded together in Opération dignité (Operation Dignity) groups and succeeded to a large extent in blocking the plans of the State. The spirit of

the Opération dignité groups is still in evidence today in the struggle agains the closing of rural post offices.

7. The Association pour la défense des droits sociaux (Association for the Defense of Social Rights) was, in the Seventies, an important organization of grassroots welfare rights groups. Some of the struggles led by this group were epic, for example the fight against the Montréal water tax. The Front commun des assistées sociales et assistés sociaux du Québec (Common Front of Welfare Recipients of Québec) has now replaced the ADDS as the umbrella organization of welfare rights groups.

8. The coops are cooperative stores run by their users. They belong to a federation that, in the mid-Seventies, included about seventy-five groups. Today, they are less popular but more diversified, with some, for example, specializing in natural foods.

9. Amitié service troisième age (Seniors' Friendship and Service) was set up in the Montréal working-class neighbourhood of Hochelaga-Maisonneuve, while Place Vermeil is in the south-central area of the city. With regard to the policy of home care for the aged, these two organizations are more progressive than any government programme.

10. The Front d'action politique (Political Action Front) included people involved both in popular groups and unions. Organized by social animators, FRAP never recovered from the repression it suffered during the October Crisis.

11. For more about this painful period in Québec history, see contemporary newspapers and books such as *FLQ: Histoire d'un mouvement clandestin* by Louis Fournier (Montréal: Québec-Amérique, 1982).

12. The Centres locaux de services communautaires (Local Community Service Centres) are neighbourhood health and social service institutions under the ministry of health and social services.

13. Translators' note: "The Quiet Revolution" is the name given to the period of massive modernization that began in the early Sixties and lasted about a decade.

14. Québec popular organizations and unions celebrate May 1 as International Workers' Day.

15. This organization has been in existence for a long time. There are almost six hundred active groups in Québec. Once identified with Catholic orthodoxy and political conservatism, the AFEAS groups now play an increasingly important role in campaigns for recognition of the economic value of housework, inclusion of women in the Québec Pension Plan, and wages for housewives.

16. The Regroupement des Centres de Femmes was founded in 1984. It currently brings together seventy-five centres involved in information, education, and social action for women.

17. The Regroupement des Maisons d'Hébergement is an association of shelters for battered women. They are funded primarily by the State, which has officially recognized the need for such services.

18. The Association québécoise pour la défense des droits des retraité-e-s et pré-retraité-e-s (Québec Association for the Rights of the Retired) is an organization of people fifty-five years of age and older. It was set up in the Eighties and is ideologically similar to the Grey Power movement. It counts dozens of local groups. With the population aging rapidly, the AQDR could become one of the most significant pressure groups of the Nineties.

Two

PEOPLE, COMMUNITIES, INTEREST GROUPS, AND ORGANIZATIONS INVOLVED IN COMMUNITY ACTION

A Few Ideological Principles

Involvement in community organizing implies an awareness of exploitation and oppression. Community organizing is based primarily on the conviction that people are capable of finding solutions to their problems. This in no way negates the often indispensable role of "experts," but it means that experts can best contribute by supporting initiatives democratically decided upon by people who have joined together to get their needs met, their rights respected, or their interests protected.

Democracy, with its recognition of people as subjects and respect for their integrity, is an essential value in community organizing. This means that community organizing involves not only strategic goals, but also the educational goal of letting people use their talents and acquire the knowledge and skills needed to carry out their projects.

Community organizing has its own values and practices. For example, organizers must be flexible about their own schedules in order to maximize the participation of the members of the group. They should also allow the pace of the work to be set by the members. We will later look more closely at the essentials of organizing a group and conducting a research project or a struggle. At this point, we merely emphasize that "professional" organizers should be aware before becoming involved in the field that it makes particular demands.

Organizers

In Québec, organizers in three categories have traditionally been involved in developing strategies of community organizing. Some have been based in institutions, but most have worked independently. The first are the progressive clergy. Educated in the doctrines of liberation theology, these members of the clergy were, and still are, involved with welfare recipients, young people, women, the peace movement, and international solidarity groups. Action in urban neighbourhoods and in certain rural areas has received a major stimulus from members of the progressive clergy, such as Jacques Couture[1] in southwest Montréal and the late Adolphe Proulx, Bishop of Hull. Opération dignité groups in the Gaspé Peninsula and the Lower St-Lawrence region received considerable help from members of the local clergy, and priests such as Jacques Grand'Maison have given generously of their time for community work. Finally, we should mention that for several years Québec religious communities have contributed financially to the support of popular organizations.

The second category of organizers consists of people trained in social work or the social sciences. Members of this group have been active since the early days of social animation. Having chosen an activist role, these organizers have played a significant part in the development of different forms of community organizing over the last quarter-century. Strongly influenced by socialism, they account for a large proportion of the organizers active in the major community organizations in Québec today.

The work of "professional" organizers has contributed to the training of large numbers of individuals who, in spite of often limited formal education, have developed their natural abilities and have become community leaders. They constitute the third category of organizers.

All three categories can be found in the organizations we will be discussing. They work in conditions that are sometimes reasonable, but more often difficult, prey to the limitations and vagaries of State funding, subject to all sorts of petty controls. Most disgraceful of all is the precariousness of their jobs, particularly in view of the contribution their work makes to society as a whole.

For some, community organizing is a livelihood. They work either in institutions or in autonomous, self-managed groups. The constraints on organizing vary depending on whether or not one is employed by the State. For example, any organizing done by employees of a CLSC (Local Community Service Centre) must fall within the institution's programmes and respect its priorities. This places considerable limitations on action. With the role of certain State apparatuses in health and social services — in particular CLSCs — currently the subject of a major debate, it seems obvious that the employees of these institutions will have less and less room in which to manoeuvre. In fact, recent statements by the minister of health and social services indicate clearly that the government would like community organizers employed by CLSCs to stop working in certain areas.[2]

Certainly the current climate favours a "community approach" — a much-vaunted concept but one that is still ill-defined. However, community organizing should not be allowed to become an excuse for the State to transfer responsibilities it no longer wants to volunteer community groups, and then to use its employees to supervise the volunteer work. Furthermore, such bureaucratic controls are totally incompatible with the ethics of community organizing.

In spite of this, however, government employees can still play an important and useful role in community organizing. Two examples are the recent work of some employees of the Seigneurie de Beauharnois CLSC in the fight to get the State to provide safe drinking water for residents of Valleyfield, and current work in the area of housing by organizers for the Buckingham CLSC in the Ottawa Valley. It is important for State employees to be completely open with the people with whom they are working about the constraints imposed by their situation, thus making sure that things are clear from the start.

There are also paid organizers working for some four thousand local community groups and their Québec-wide federations. The constraints imposed on them differ substantially from those experienced by their colleagues working for the State. Unlike government employment, their jobs and working conditions tend to be precarious. Most are not unionized, and they can be subjected to the arbitrary exercise of power by groups that do not follow the rules of democracy. Since autonomous groups are funded primarily by State programmes, their existence is very much influenced by decisions to retain or abolish these programmes. This has created a climate of insecurity and has forced groups to be constantly on the lookout for funding. It is estimated that staff members of community organizations spend twenty-five percent of their time "running after funding." Another common condition of community group employees is that they are expected to do a certain amount of unpaid work alongside volunteer activists. Finally, most community groups are not able to offer the range of fringe benefits enjoyed by State employees, such as overtime pay, retirement plans, parental leave, and training allowances.

The most important difference between paid organizers and activists or volunteers is the greater availability and heavier workload of the former. Paid organizers are also likely to be better informed about the group's activities. This puts them in a position to exert undue influence on decisions, something they should be careful to avoid.

Still another distinction is that members tend to unload their responsibilities on the staff. You could be hit with the phrase "You do it, that's what you're paid for," when you least expect it. Another consequence of being a paid organizer rather than an unpaid activist is the ever-present risk that your activities serve more to justify your job than to advance the interests and objectives of the group. This tendency is even stronger when jobs are scarce. A related danger is that of putting your own interests as an employee before those of the group. Employees of an organization, for example, may oppose providing the financial support needed by volunteers, such as reimbursement of childcare and transportation costs, because it would take away from the funds available for salaries. Far be it from us to do anything to make the working conditions of staff in these groups any more difficult, but we must emphasize that volunteers should also be able to count on a minimum of financial resources.

Employees of some federations have demanded salaries equal to those of their State counterparts. Such demands cannot be justified without first considering the employees of the groups affiliated to these federations, whose working conditions are usually even worse. As a general rule, community groups and organizations do not try to exploit their employees, but working conditions cannot approach those of the private sector or government. You should be aware of this before you apply. On the other hand, working for a community organization offers definite compensations — the freedom to set your own schedule, the feeling of being socially useful, and the satisfaction of seeing progress made. Finally, the experience of solidarity with people in struggle can be very rewarding.

An organization's staff plays a decisive political role. Normally, it is the staff who speak for the group in meetings with representatives of the State. They also participate in meetings to organize common fronts, coalitions, and other collaborative activities, and routinely represent the group in lobbying. Too often, employees schedule activities for their group at times when it is impossible for many members to attend — for example, holding conferences on weekdays, when most volunteers are busy with jobs or family responsibilities.

We feel that one of the major roles of paid staff should be educational. They should put as much effort as possible into training the members themselves to represent the group. Employees should be flexible about scheduling activities and allocating resources in order to encourage membership participation. Employees of popular organizations cannot function like civil servants. We emphasize this point because we see an increasing tendency in Québec-wide organizations for employees to take the leadership. This role should be shared with the elected representatives of the membership.

Activists

Activists have a special place in the popular movement. Their role is central and indispensable. Without them, a group dissolves or becomes something more like a State institution or a private organization. The development of the popular movement and the establishment of a growing number of Québec-wide federations have made it necessary to rethink the role of activists.

Activism means acting and fighting for the values in which one believes. It means being willing to sacrifice peace and comfort for the benefit of others. Activism in the popular movement is a form of generosity on the part of thousands of Québecers. It is not the same as being active in a union or a political party, because the popular movement has its own unique dynamics. Activism can mean performing humble tasks such as answering the telephone, running the office, speaking for the group, or participating in workshops. It frequently means being involved in a struggle. The Montréal welfare recipients' fight against the municipal water tax, the struggle of young people in RAJ,[3] the fight against racism, the struggle of the handicapped, and that of women against violence and pornography are all made possible by the activism of thousands of individuals.

In the Eighties, a certain petty-bourgeoisie element that had been active in the Seventies took it upon itself to put activism on trial. The collapse of the organizations calling themselves Marxist-Leninist, the defeat of the referendum on Québec independence, and the ideological shift of the Parti québécois led some to proclaim the death of activism. Analysis shows, however, that while activism may have gone through a lull — this also occurred after the October Crisis in 1970 — it has not died. Clearly, though, activism today takes different forms. It is more modest, and big demonstrations are less popular than they were in the Sixties and Seventies. But activism is still the cornerstone of community organizing.

In our encounters with activists from popular groups and community organizations, many spoke of the difficulties of activism. There are two kinds of problems. First, there are the financial problems that all organizations experience to one degree or another, and the problem of participation. Second, some activists feel they are not always sufficiently involved in decision-making processes. Communication problems between Québec-wide federations and their member groups, and a lack of information often discourage participation by members. These questions will be dealt with more fully below, but we feel they deserve mention here.

Community organizing strategies should be planned with a view to promoting active participation, and a substantial portion of the group's resources should be allocated to supporting it. Organizations that fail to do so risk losing the backing that is essential to their very existence. In concrete terms, the test of a popular organization is its capacity to generate activist involvement. A good network of activists increases a group's possibilities. It is also an effective antidote to the repression sometimes exercised against groups that are too militant in the eyes of the powers-that-be.

Members

The membership of a group consists of all those who have made the decision to belong. They are not all activists, but their number is a measure of the group's vitality and to some extent an indication of its political strength. Some associations, such as AFEAS (Associations féminines d'Éducation et d'Action sociale), have memberships numbering in the tens of thousands. Others, like the Association québecoise pour la défense des droits des retraité-e-s et pré-retraité-e-s (AQDR - Québec Association for the Rights of the Retired), draw on a smaller pool of members but one that belongs to a more activist tradition. Depending on the nature of the group, the membership may be made up of individuals, of individuals and institutions, or of local groups, as in the case with Québec-wide federations. The latter include the Fédération des Centres d'Action bénévole du Québec (Québec Federation of Volunteer Centres),[4] the Regroupement des Centres de Femmes (Federation of Women's Centres), and the Regroupement des Maisons d'Hébergement (Federation of Women's Shelters).

We will discuss only individual members since all groups and organizations ultimately depend on the membership of individuals. It is important, however, to mention that the individuals designated by organizations to take part in the community organizing activities of other groups are normally answerable to those from whom they have received their mandate. This situation can lead to ideological conflicts or conflicts of interest. This has occurred, for example, with union representatives in peace and disarmament coalitions.

According to the democratic principles of the popular movement, the general meeting of the membership of a group has supreme authority. It is the members who decide orientations, approve strategy, ratify reports, authorize changes to statutes and bylaws, and take major political decisions.

While not all members are militant activists, it is from the membership that the activists are recruited. Furthermore, a member who for a time is inactive may eventually become more involved. The important thing to remember is that the members should be the first to know what is happening in the organization. Every effort should be made to keep them informed and involved, because they have shown by joining the organization that they are interested in its activities.

Not only should the members be consulted as much as possible, but their opinions must always be respected and their decisions followed. It can be frustrating for paid staff and activists when the membership is not in agreement with everything they propose. For those involved in the action on a daily basis, the temptation to disregard decisions of the general meeting or recommendations of committees can be strong, but to do so is a serious mistake and can compromise an organization's credibility. Democratic values are essential to community organization. Collective action is based on the belief that democracy depends on the involvement of individuals and collectivities. This belief carries with it the obligation to see that our organizations are as democratic as possible in their own internal functioning.

Where Organizing Takes Place

The concept of community

The concept of community is often confused with that of geographical area, but the distinction is important. An area is a specific physical place with all its specific characteristics. A neighbourhood, a town, a region, a country, each has its own distinct character. The importance of place is evident in our everyday language: we say we work "in St-Henri," "in the Lower St. Lawrence region," or "in Hochelaga-Maisonneuve." When we speak of community, we add to the concept of area the concept of population. The population of an area constitutes the community. In this book, we prefer to speak of the local community, since it more closely links the human and geographic dimensions of the setting in which organizing takes place.

Our awareness and definition of social problems are most often based on the local community. There is a tendency today to look at questions concerning community action from a less locally-oriented perspective. The women's movement and organizations of welfare recipients and the unemployed approach their respective issues from the broader perspective of the social stratum concerned. The development beyond localism is positive, but an organizer still has to work in a specific setting, with a population identified with a geographical area. In the following sections, we will describe briefly the main types of communities in which organizers work.

Working-class neighbourhoods

The social reality of the neighbourhood is clearly expressed in the concept of *la petite patrie* ("little nation") popularized by writer Claude

Jasmin[5] and successfully used by Jacques Couture in his campaign for mayor of Montréal. The neighbourhood is a multidimensional reality that can be looked at from the point of view of history, geography, or local culture. Partly objective and partly subjective, the idea of neighbourhood is solidly anchored in the experience of people who live in urban settings. While neighbourhood life was once expected to crumble under the repeated attacks of land speculators, it seems now, ironically, to have undergone a revival.

Before embarking on action, organizers are well advised to learn about the history of the neighbourhood and to make sure they understand the processes that have determined its physical boundaries and its unique character.

The notion of class has only relatively recently been applied to neighbourhoods. What we call "working-class" neighbourhoods were not very long ago called "underprivileged." This change in terminology is related to a shift in ideology among organizers. "Underprivileged neighbourhood" reflects a Christian perspective on community action, a view involving "the big people and the little people," "the privileged and the underprivileged." The critique of urban social animation that led to the founding of the Front d'action politique (FRAP) in Montréal also led to a change from the use of "underprivileged neighbourhood" to "working-class neighbourhood," a term that has very different ideological connotations and that is more appropriate politically. A working-class neighbourhood might be concisely defined as one in which ordinary working people live. This idea of the working-class neighbourhood as opposed to the bourgeois neighbourhood is a Marxist concept because it sees reality in terms of social classes and their distinct cultures. In spite of their individual differences, working-class neighbourhoods are all made up of a majority of workers, welfare recipients, the unemployed, the elderly and the young, and a minority of petty bourgeois, which includes artists and organizers. They are also marked by high population density, lack of green space, and proximity to expressways and main thoroughfares.

Each working-class neighbourhood has its own particular history. Hochelaga-Maisonneuve, for example, was two independent municipalities before being amalgamated into Montréal, and St-Henri and Pointe St-Charles were once villages. Each has been marked by its history, particularly its industrial history. St-Henri was once known for its tanneries, and the construction of the Lachine Canal made the southwest of Montréal, in the not-so-distant past, one of Canada's main industrial centres. The development of the east end of Montréal was based on heavy industry and oil refineries. These factors have profoundly influenced the cultures of the communities in these areas of the city. Working-class neighbourhoods also have their own traditions related to community action, and it was in these neighbourhoods that the first experiments in community organizing took place.

Working-class neighbourhoods have undergone profound transformation, and some have been almost totally demolished. The south central area of Montréal lost a large expanse known as the *faubourg à m'lasse ("molasses town")* [6] to make room for the Canadian Broadcasting Corporation building. The construction of the Université du Québec à Montréal and several large development projects also had profound effects on the neighbourhood. As a result of these physical changes, the social fabric of the community, which had been homogeneous, became very diverse. While part of the original population remained, the south central area was invaded by university students, media people and bureaucrats from the Canadian Broadcasting Corporation and Radio-Québec, and employees from the new office towers. The neighbourhood remains working class, but it has undergone enormous changes.

The same phenomenon is occurring in Québec City with the construction of several big government buildings, as well as in Hull, Trois-Rivières, and Sherbrooke. The uncontrolled development of cities, under the influence of speculators and their allies in city halls and other levels of government, has resulted in profound changes to the physical space and the social fabric of many working-class neighbourhoods.

Another result has been the proletarianization of other neighbourhoods as populations are displaced from the city core to surrounding areas. When people are forced out of their neighbourhoods, they have to be housed somewhere. The old "underprivileged" neighbourhoods of Montréal are still working-class, but there are now many others as well.

Any analysis of the changes in the social fabric of the city must also take into account the evolution of social classes. Economic recession and technological change have resulted in the proletarianization of sectors of the population that were once considered part of the petty bourgeoisie. Extended unemployment among university graduates, layoffs of teachers, factory closings, and increases in the numbers of single-parent families have all affected the structure of communities.

Many residents of working-class neighbourhoods have literally been evicted from their communities, replaced by a new petty bourgeoisie able to pay higher rents. In Montréal, this gentrification has been most spectacular in the Plateau Mont-Royal area. Yet, in spite of the changes, these neighbourhoods remain working-class, and methods of organizing suited to the new populations will be added to those already developed to meet the needs of the original social groups.

Other neighbourhoods

Community organizing no longer focuses only on working-class neighbourhoods. It takes place in other neighbourhoods that could be called mixed, such as Notre-Dame-de-Grâce and Outremont. Urban renewal has not only hit the areas where working people live, as is illustrated by the damage inflicted on the Montréal neighbourhood in which Pierre Elliott Trudeau lives. Let us leave aside the problems of the unfortunate rich, however, and look at neighbourhoods that, without being working-class, still have a potential for organizing.

These neighbourhoods are relatively well-to-do, with nice houses, large amounts of green space, quiet streets, no businesses on residential streets, and quality health, education, and social service institutions. Of course, there are no factories. The population usually consists of the upper strata of the petty bourgeoisie and of a middle class that makes its money from financial institutions and the management of small and medium-sized businesses. There are also senior civil servants, politicians, and a certain number of successful artists. A close look will also reveal areas whose residents are similar to those of working-class neighbourhoods. People in these neighbourhoods tend to show greater interest in certain types of struggles, such as those involving environmental or peace issues. Many of the issues in which community organizers are involved today are not specific to any type of neighbourhood. For example, mental health problems, domestic violence, and incest are as widespread in bourgeois as in working-class neighbourhoods, and environmental pollution respects no boundaries. Community organizing must be adaptable to any type of community.

The suburbs

The suburbs have grown spectacularly over the last thirty years with the increase in our collective wealth and increasing capacity for consumption. The tens of thousands of bungalows lined up along the streets of Brossard, Laval, and Ste-Foy are testimony to the huge changes that have taken place in Québec society since the end of the second world war.

The development of the suburbs has resulted in a new distribution of population over large areas, and the need to provide new services. Many CLSCs, for example, will need to be set up to serve the suburbs. The development of suburbia has also given rise to new problems related to isolation, boredom, and the need for greater mobility.

Community groups are increasingly active in the suburbs. In the last few years, women's groups, youth centres, associations of retired people, and a multitude of other groups have been formed to deal with a range of problems. Cooperation between organizers in the cities and in the suburbs has been difficult to achieve. Yet, although the two kinds of communities are distinct, they also have common concerns, and it might be useful for them to work together on issues such as public transportation or domestic violence.

Rural areas

Community organizing strategies must be adapted to the physical organization of the territory and the social makeup of the population in rural areas. In general, the organizing base will be the town or village, or the region. While the concerns of rural people can be similar to those of people in big cities, there are also important differences. For example, welfare recipients obviously have the same basic problems in the country as in the city, but in some ways their difficulties are less acute while in others they are more so. In the country one can have a garden, pick wild fruit and vegetables, or hunt and fish for food, but transportation will probably be more of a problem. The social makeup of rural areas, in addition to the classes and social groups found in the city, also includes farmers, fishers, forestry workers, and seasonal farmworkers and workers in the tourist industry. It is not uncommon to find families who live below the poverty line owning their homes. This is rarely the case in an urban setting. Rural areas are marked by low population density and relatively great distances between towns.

City and country are also different in terms of areas of interest. An example is the mobilization of farm wives to gain recognition as full economic partners in the family enterprise, since they are as involved as their husbands in the production process. This struggle led by rural women has attracted a great deal of active support, forcing the Union des producteurs agricoles (Québec Farmers' Union) to re-examine its policies and radically challenging the "male" right to property. This kind of struggle could take place only in the country, yet these women's successes in having their rights recognized will have major repercussions on the status of women in general. Other examples of rural struggles include the mobilization of farmers against the expropriation of their land for the construction of Mirabel Airport (which was finally successful in 1988), the struggle against the damming of the Jacques-Cartier River by Hydro-Québec, and the Opération dignité groups in the Gaspé and Lower St. Lawrence region.

Organizing strategies have to take into account local characteristics, and the activities of organizations that also exist in the city have to be adapted to the regional culture. In the country, people are less in a hurry. They also tend to be closer to their employers, since they usually live in the same villages and towns; this can drastically affect the possibilities for mobilization. Power is often much more tangible in rural areas. In some villages, a single family essentially controls the local economy and is prominent in every aspect of social and political life, from social clubs and church activities to the local Caisse populaire (parish credit union), the municipal administration, federal and provincial political parties, and the school board.

In the country, your activities quickly become known and sometimes take on astonishing importance. Things that go unnoticed in the city, such as how you dress, your religious practices, how you educate your children, or your relationships, stand out in a small town. Rural areas have their own characteristics and culture, and organizers must adapt or risk failure.

Interest Groups

We feel it is important to look at the main social groups likely to be involved in any community organizing process. Writers continue to discuss the question of social classes, and new interpretations show how complex a question it still is a century after Marx's death. While we recognize the existence of two major classes with diametrically opposed interests, we can no longer accept simplistic views of the bourgeoisie and the proletariat. It is important to take into account the development of the petty bourgeoisie and the decisive role it plays in society today, with some of its component groups, such as professionals and university professors, showing corporatist tendencies and others undergoing proletarianization. Similarly, the concept of the proletariat needs to be revised to take into account the growing numbers of workers excluded from the working world or condemned to short-term or part-time jobs.

We emphasize the need for organizers to understand the interests that drive social groups in Québec, since interests dictate the choices of friends and allies in an organizing situation. Understanding the social classes and their component groups is indispensable for developing strategies.

People excluded from productive work

The current economic recession is increasing the numbers of this group and giving it more political weight than it has in times of prosperity. In 1987, there were 625,000 people in Québec living on welfare. Many of these were under thirty years of age, condemned by government policy to subsist on less than half the normal benefits. Most welfare recipients are women who head single-parent families or individuals whose unemployment benefits have run out. Many have physical or mental disabilities, and many are too young to receive old-age pensions but too old to have a reasonable chance of getting a job. In some urban neighbourhoods and some rural villages, the majority of the population lives on welfare.

Until the end of the Sixties, social animators did not believe welfare recipients were important politically. A few organizing failures were considered confirmation of their status as "sub-proletariat." This situation changed when the first ADDS groups were set up in Pointe St-Charles and Little Burgundy in Montréal. Today there are more than sixty independent groups of welfare recipients joined together in the Front commun des assistées sociales et assistés sociaux du Québec (Common Front of Québec Welfare Recipients). The success of such organizations shows the flaws in the social animators' analysis.

The second large group of people excluded from productive work are the unemployed, one rung above welfare recipient on the poverty ladder. The unemployed are harder to organize than people on welfare, probably because they still hope to go back to work. The newspaper headlines, however, tell a lot about their real chances of finding employment. Things have reached the point where even young engineers and administrators, so in demand a few years ago, have joined the ranks of the unemployed. Although they are difficult to mobilize, the unemployed have set up organizations and services, such as the Mouvement Action-Chômage (Unemployment Action Movement). During the Great Depression of the Thirties the unemployed were a major political force, and the marches they organized are famous to this day.

A third category of people excluded from the working world has developed as a result of the attack on working conditions over the last decade. A growing number of people are today condemned to working for wages no higher than unemployment and welfare benefits. These "vagabonds of dreams," as they have been poetically described, are often well educated. They work as university lecturers, as supply teachers, on short-term contracts in health and social services, and fill other marginal functions in institutions, and they are sometimes employed by grass-roots community organizations and State job-creation projects. Every year there are more and more of these people pushed to the margins of the system by the combined effects of corporatism and privatization. A large proportion of the progressive community and as well as many cultural workers belong to this new proletariat.

Women

It has become commonplace that women make up the majority of the popular movement. Yet there was a time when groups and organizations were almost always led by men. In the union movement women are still in the minority in the leadership. Fortunately, things are beginning to change, and this change must be taken into account in community organizing. Groups should adopt policies to encourage the participation of women, such as providing childcare during activities and taking into account the double workload of women employed outside the home.

It is not our place to detail the many demands put forward by the women's movement and by women active in the union and popular movements. We should, however, point out the exceptional contribution women have made to the progressive forces in society, a contribution that has taken many forms. Women's demands with regard to family violence, pornography, sexual stereotyping, equality in employment and pay, equal participation in economic and political life, sharing of responsibility for domestic tasks and child rearing, medical practices, and reproductive technology have all raised issues that are important for our collective ethics.

Feminist activists have also established a very important network of independent groups that deal with many aspects of women's oppression. There are about fifteen federations and coalitions, including the Regroupement des centres de femmes (Federation of Women's Centres), which has close to seventy-five member groups, the Regroupement des Maisons d'Hébergement (Federation of Women's Shelters), made up of about fifty groups, the AFEAS groups with some 650 clubs, the Centres de santé des femmes (Women's Health Centres), and the Québec Women's Federation. These organizations are in contact with hundreds of thousands of women every year, providing them with indispensable services. There are also groups working in theatre, film, and video production, and publishing houses that put out books by women active in community organizing.

The strong presence of women, both in mixed organizations and in their own groups, has had a major impact on community organizing. The feminist critique of group process in the Sixties and Seventies has changed how groups operate and has to some extent — although still insufficiently — revitalized democracy in organizations. For example, the leadership of many organizations is much more balanced now, and in some federations, such as the federation of ACEFs (Associations coopératives d'économie familiale — Cooperative Family Budget Associations), female staff predominate. No organizer today can afford to underestimate the importance of women or fail to take their needs into account.

Young people

Not a day goes by without something being said about the problems of young people. There has been a strong tendency to marginalize the young, to push them off into their own corner. Much of the world of young people consists of structures and values established by their elders. Often they instinctively reject a world they did not make.

Young people are hardly represented at decision-making levels of the popular movement, as if they were the farthest thing from its concerns. Yet, as we have seen, young people are prime victims of unemployment, discriminatory welfare laws, and consumer problems. Some groups, such as the ADDS and the Mouvement

Action-Chômage, have made a special effort to mobilize young people, and they deserve to be commended. On the other hand, government programmes that aim to get young people involved in volunteer work or underpaid jobs should be regarded with suspicion.

In the last few years, there has been a resurgence of youth organizations. Although the student movement seems unable to mobilize its troops and the Regroupement autonome des Jeunes (Autonomous Youth Organization) has dissolved as a result of internal conflicts, other forms of organizing with young people have proven more effective, particularly during the last five years. The network of youth centres has expanded and shelters have been opened in order to provide minimal resources for homeless young people. Groups have formed to protest discriminatory welfare policies, and in the unions the problems of young people are becoming a priority, at least in convention resolutions.

But the conditions of a large proportion of young people have continually deteriorated over the last several years. The problems of homelessness, drug addiction, prostitution, unemployment, school dropouts, and family violence have become major social issues and should give rise to new initiatives in community organizing.

The working class

The working class is not monolithic, and while everyone in it shares the same objective interests, there are also important differences. Often, idealistic organizers behave as if the simple fact of producing goods gives a worker a certificate of virtue. Lack of judgement in assessing the realities of the working class can lead to serious errors in organizing.

First, it should be emphasized that the upper segment of the working class, which Marxists call the "labour aristocracy," is especially susceptible to the bourgeois mirage. Although sociologically and economically they are exploited in their labour, they have a very limited consciousness of their exploitation, particularly if they have been seduced by the "American dream."

The working class also has marked reactionary tendencies with regard to the most oppressed classes. Many in the labour aristocracy consider welfare recipients nothing more than parasites and incurable alcoholics. They say the unemployed are lazy, and that young people should have to do military service or some other kind of compulsory service. These workers are also exploited, and subjected to a different kind of oppression. In times of recession they are hit by unemployment, and since they have more to lose than the majority of workers, they are harder hit. Most of them are unionized, and they are generally very combative when it comes to defending their economic interests against the big corporations that employ them.

This segment of the working class belongs to the most heavily taxed part of the population. This is certainly a form of oppression and can be an excellent starting point for mobilization, as was shown by the tax revolt in California a few years ago and in Québec in the movement of opposition to increases in property taxes in many municipalities.

The majority of workers work for relatively low — often extremely low wages — in companies that are frequently not in good financial health. In industries such as confectionery and textiles, many are paid the minimum wage. Large numbers work on a seasonal basis. The threat of unemployment always hangs over their heads, and in times of economic stagnation, this threat is even more effective because of the abundance of available labour.

Unionized or not, most workers are exploited and oppressed. The unionized segment of the working class is the group with the highest level of consciousness and the one with which other oppressed segments of society have the most interest in allying themselves. Any community organizing should take into account the natural links between the popular movement and the union movement. These links are expressed not only in large gatherings like the Sommet populaire (Popular Summit),[7] but on all kinds of occasions. The union movement should be considered a group's best ally in community action, even though — particularly since the beginning of the Eighties — large segments of it have lapsed into corporatism, looking out only for their own interests. One of the most important tasks today is to develop conditions for creative cooperation between the union movement and the popular movement in order to hold onto important social rights jeopardized by the reorientation of the welfare state towards increased support for the private sector.

Popular groups and unions

In Québec, at least until the Eighties, there was a tradition of the popular movement and the union movement working closely together, often joining forces on major issues. Unfortunately, over the last few years, union federations have tended more and more to withdraw into themselves, and expressions of solidarity have become rarer and largely symbolic.

From the Sixties up to the mid-Seventies, cooperation between the unions and the popular movement took many forms. Unions got involved in the struggle for better living conditions, giving their support to consumer groups and welfare rights groups. The union movement also took stands on a number of issues of general interest in the area of housing, the minimum wage, automobile insurance, daycare, education, and health and social services. It has also played an important role in women's fight for equality. During the big demonstrations against wage controls in the mid-Seventies, members of popular groups marched side-by-side with trade-unionists. Retired people and welfare recipients also came out in support of striking workers during the 1975 asbestos strike and the 1974 postal strike.

There was also cooperation in politics. To some extent, the Parti québécois brought together activists from popular groups and the union movement. The Front d'action politique (FRAP), which took on the entrenched municipal administration in the Montréal election of 1970, was the joint creation of union federations and popular groups. The same can be said of the Montréal Citizens' Movement, now in power at city hall. The Mouvement socialiste[8] and the New Democratic Party are also led by activists from these two movements.

With the economic recession of the late Seventies, the union movement seemed to turn inward. It can no longer be assumed that unions and popular groups are on the same wavelength, although they are still capable of forming common fronts, as we saw recently in the fight against the Québec government's repressive proposals for welfare reform. Activists in the popular movement have become more and more critical of the unions, accusing them of corporatism. At the same time, workers are less receptive to the concerns of popular groups. A link has been broken that urgently needs to be restored. Recent initiatives such as the creation of Solidarité Populaire Québec may prove helpful in re-establishing cooperation.

New areas may offer possibilities for rebuilding solidarity between the union and popular movements. Environmental concerns, women's issues, and the language question are opportunities to develop positions that are, if not common, at least very close. In other areas, such as disarmament or health and social service reform, finding common ground may prove more difficult.

Solidarity between unions and popular groups is particularly essential now, when the State is becoming more and more clearly identified with the interests of capital, promoting private enterprise, and cutting back in areas that affect the quality of life of large numbers of people. In this context, it is in the interest of the popular movement and the union movement to unite against the forces threatening them both. With the widespread erosion of job security and social rights, the stakes are too high for progressive elements not to make the effort to identify their common interests and build on them to create solidarity. This is an essential aspect of community organizing today.

The petty bourgeoisie

There was a time — perhaps not yet past — when it was an insult to call someone "petty bourgeois." Belonging to the petty bourgeoisie put a stigma on a community organizer. Strangely enough, most organizers came from petty-bourgeois origins. While it is no longer in fashion to attack people for their class background, community organizing is still a field for graduates in social work or other social science disciplines. This is not cause for alarm. On the contrary, it is a good thing that women and men with the kind of education that could guarantee them a comfortable place in society choose to work to change society. This choice implies that they have questioned their own privilege and have reached a certain level of consciousness. People generally appreciate it when a lawyer, a social worker, a community organizer, an artist, or an architect chooses to live in solidarity with the oppressed classes of society. They do not take offense, but instead take advantage of the skills and knowledge these petty bourgeois have to offer.

It must be noted, however, that there is a tendency among petty bourgeois to defend their own interests, and their interests are not always compatible with those of the women and men in the popular and union movements. The minority of the petty bour-geoisie that defends working-class interests is, in a way, the counterpart of the minority of the working class that aligns itself with the bourgeoisie. Writers such as Gramsci have studied these phenomena.

There are members of the petty bourgeoisie at every level of the State, in all areas of political and social life. In community action, you will inevitably have to negotiate with them. It is important to under-stand them in order to know how far to collaborate with them. We must not forget the petty-bourgeois tendency to co-optation. How many ideas were cultivated in the gardens of the working class only to be reaped by the State for the benefit of petty-bourgeois technocrats and bureaucrats! Yet, even with its corporatist tendencies, the petty bourgeoisie can, in certain circumstances, be an ally of the popular movement.

The local elite

Popular groups often find themselves pitted against a local elite made up of small merchants, professionals, clergy, election or-ganizers, and local politicians. They are particularly important be-cause they control the organizations on which groups are more or less dependent for funding and legitimacy. The history of the popular movement is full of examples of struggles between local populations and these local "establishments."

The local elite is the natural ally of the bourgeoisie, but it can also aid in the development of certain groups. Alliances with the local elite are always extremely fragile and require a good deal of tact on the part of the organizer. We will discuss this subject further in the chapters on researching the community.

Those who control the means of production

These are the real bosses. They are the principal power that both the union movement and the popular movement are up against. Their interests, to put it generously, are not easily reconcilable with the interests of the people with whom we work. Their ethics are evident in their public statements. In the debate over the much-publicized Canadian bishops' letter on the State's economic choices, for example, they clearly expressed their absolute faith in the private appropriation of the fruits of the labour of others.

Those who control the means of production are the true masters of society. They have all the rights, including the right to special treatment by the justice system. They influence the lawmakers in their favour. It is their ideology that demands the dismantling of the mechanisms for the redistribution of wealth, the withdrawal of funding from social services, keeping the minimum wage down, conscripting young people, welfare recipients, and the unemployed, and limiting women's rights and access to paid work. They are the force popular groups come up against every time they demand that their rights be respected or broadened. They know very well that the organized strength of working people and of the oppressed classes in the unions and popular movements constitutes the only real threat to their hold on power. Organizers must always be aware of this.

Politicians

Sooner or later, anyone who gets involved in community work will meet a politician, or, at the very least, negotiate with one through an intermediary. Organizers should be aware that a politician's main concern is get elected or re-elected. It is therefore important to let him or her know how representative your group is of the population of the riding, and how much influence your membership has in the area.

Any contact with politicians or their representatives requires tact and diplomacy. There is no point in burning your bridges before you cross them. Politicians are often amenable to simple arguments, the kind of arguments they themselves might use with voters. On the whole, they like to be of service; it appeals to their paternalistic instincts and makes them feel important. Most politicians are not academics, nor are most of them millionaires. They are usually notaries, lawyers, businessmen, ex-union organizers, former teachers, or other members of the petty bourgeoisie. Most are just ordinary backbenchers, cabinet posts being reserved for a select few.

You will meet some politicians who think that all community workers are dangerous agitators, but these are in the minority. Most know that you aren't dangerous, and that, in fact, you help maintain a certain balance in a rapidly changing world. Usually, you will be contacting them about a grant. They will be charming, obliging, understanding, and perhaps even willing to give it to you. If they do, they will ensure that this is made known. Given the climate of Québec-Canada rivalry, they will even want you to put up a sign indicating the source of the grant at the entrance to your office.

You may meet your elected representative under more difficult circumstances, during an occupation of his or her office, for example. In such a situation, the politician will be nervous, make promises, and, above all, remember your name.

Whatever reasons you have for contacting elected representatives or other politicians, never meet them alone. Always go with one or more members of your group. Commitments made by politicians are worth more when they are made in front of several people.

Experience with the Parti québécois and, more recently, the Montréal Citizens' Movement, shows that relationships with politicians are not the same when they are in power as when they are in opposition. This demonstrates how important it is for groups involved in community organizing to maintain their independence with regard to political parties. Sooner or later, whatever party is in power, the popular movement is likely to find itself opposing its policies and its programmes. It has become clear that professional politicians, even those that claim to be social democrats, are governed by partisan interests and electoral considerations that are contrary to the interests of the popular movement. It is therefore best to be cautious in relations with political parties. This is not to say that you should refuse to have anything to do with them, only that you set clear limits on the cooperation you request and the tactical support you offer.

Technocrats

The technocrats are the people who really run the State. They can be roughly divided into two groups: political appointees directly connected with the party in power, who are likely to lose their jobs with a change in government; and the others — who are much more numerous — who administer State institutions such as CLSCs, CSSs, and adult education programmes.

What distinguishes this interest group, with the partial exception of the first category, is that they are not answerable to the electorate. They are therefore less responsive to some kinds of arguments and more responsive to others. They are most amenable to rational argument. They like to hear figures and see demonstrations. They can appreciate a serious project, and will often have enough social consciousness to take certain risks with individuals they see as competent. On the other hand, they abhor anyone who does not respect hierarchies. In your dealings with technocrats, make sure you know your facts and figures well, since they usually know theirs.

Sometimes technocrats hide behind ministerial directives. This was the case in some of the welfare recipients' struggles. In these instances, it may be useful to know the actual contents of the directive and, preferably, to obtain a copy. As with politicians, it is always better to go as a group when dealing with a technocrat.

Settings for Community Organizing

Local Community Service Centres
(CLSCs — Centres locaux de services communautaires)

The Quiet Revolution, as the pivotal events of the Sixties in Québec are called, was a period of structural transformation of the State apparatus. Education reform was at the centre of the changes, since other reforms were impossible until the State had qualified personnel to take on the administration of new and modernized services. The second important area of reform was health and social services, where it was carried out in the name of efficiency and participation. The participation aspect of the reform was an early indication of the role that community workers would be called on to play.

The opening of the first CLSCs in the early Seventies was preceded by intense mobilization around the issues of health, social services, and the organization of community life. Community centres and community clinics were set up in working-class neighbourhoods, including St-Jacques, Pointe St-Charles, St-Henri, and Hochelaga-Maisonneuve in Montréal. These community services were original in that they were profoundly democratic, controlled by the population and managed by its elected representatives. The general meeting of users set their policies and priorities and decided which types of services should be emphasized. Most provided free prescription drugs, an appropriate practice in neighbourhoods where people would have had to cut back on essentials to buy medicine. A great deal of emphasis was placed on prevention. Nutrition was singled out as a priority and dietitians were hired to provide education. These clinics and community centres were set up by grass-roots groups, and area residents got involved in them as they did in the many other committees set up to improve conditions in their neighbourhoods.

An important feature of the community clinics was the high level of consciousness among their employees. Professionals accepted salaries equivalent to those of the average worker. Many doctors, in particular, voluntarily turned over to the clinics hundreds of thousands of dollars that would have gone into their own pockets as medicare fees. Community action was particularly important in these clinics, and almost everyone was involved in popular education or struggles. As part of their communities, the clinics provided support for the struggles of other groups. All this could not last.

Co-optation is not painless. Communities resisted. The State responded with threats of budget cuts. Finally, one by one, the community clinics surrendered, although a few have managed to maintain some of their uniqueness.

In response to the government's announced intention to entrust the management of CLSCs to representatives of the community, and attracted by the new possibilities of work in these institutions, community organizers in many working-class neighbourhoods mobilized people to form implementation committees for the new CLSCs. Many groups agreed to take part in these committees. They saw them as adding a new dimension to their activities and as an opportunity to work toward the establishment of services that were desperately needed. Study after study, complete with figures, charts, and diagrams, clearly demonstrated that people living in working-class neighbourhoods were more susceptible to certain diseases, such as tuberculosis. These efforts were rewarded with budgets to set up the new institutions.

The CLSCs are a prime example of State co-optation of a popular initiative. They also show the idealism of the many organizers who believed in the possibility of community control of services set up by the State. There is much to be learned from the experience of organizers involved in setting up CLSCs, even though we feel CLSCs are basically a positive development in the field of health and social services.

The first lesson for organizers is the need to understand the nature of the State and the constraints it puts on community work. Secondly, the decision to work in support of State initiatives should always be explained in a frank discussion with the people with whom one is working. Many people mobilized in the CLSC implementation committees believed the promise of participation and community control. When they saw the power fall into the hands of the technocrats, their disenchantment seriously affected their willingness to participate in further community activities. The disappointment turned into disillusionment and cynicism when they saw those who had mobilized them being hired by these institutions at salaries beyond their own reach. This no doubt explains the extreme mistrust of organizers paid by the State shown by activists and members of popular groups. You reap what you sow.

CLSCs today employ many community workers, some as community organizers, others as social workers, and a few as health professionals. Most salaried community workers work in CLSCs. The limits of their activities are set by the management of the institutions paying their salaries. It is possible, in this situation, to offer valuable services to the community, provided one is aware of the limits. Popular groups fighting for the rights of workers injured on the job, for example, owe their existence to community organizers from a CLSC. Some CLSC social workers work with tenants' rights groups, and others are active with women's groups. Youth, the elderly, environmental protection, and consumerism are other areas in which CLSC community workers can be active.

In the last few years, CLSCs have come under serious criticism. Although their existence is no longer threatened, many ministerial statements have insisted that their mandate be redefined. Since publication of the Brunet, Harnois, and Rochon Commission reports,[9] the Federation of CLSCs seems to have accepted a narrowing of the role of CLSCs. It appears that in coming years there will be a withdrawal of funding from more socially oriented activities, and increased emphasis on health. The process of reorientation the CLSCs are currently undergoing is accompanied by expressions of official approval of the "community approach." However, it is still difficult to understand just what CLSC leaders mean by this term. In spite of all this uncertainty, CLSC employees are, in general, important resource persons for groups involved in community organizing. In Part 2 we will discuss the implications of being a State employee when organizing a struggle.

Social Service Centres[10]

One of the main questions inherent in the practice of social work is whether to organize or to provide "band-aids." Employees of Social Service Centres are hired to do casework. Any involvement in community work is considered extraneous to their jobs and can be pursued only on a voluntary basis. Yet social work provides rare insights into human misery, and knowledge that can be very useful to popular groups. For example, a social worker working with physically and psychologically abused women could join forces with a women's group involved in fighting this oppression.

Adult education

Like CLSCs and Social Service Centres, adult education programmes can serve as a basis for community organizing. Here again, the point is not to replace voluntary community organizations in the field, but rather to provide them with technical support. Community organizing and popular education are historically connected. People who work for adult education programmes can give groups valuable assistance in obtaining grants and technical resources. They can also hinder their progress with red tape. We will discuss adult education programmes further in the section on funding.

Citizens' groups

We have already looked at the origins of citizens' groups in the history section of this book. The term "citizens' group" was used to refer to a group of individuals under the tutelage of a social animator. Citizens' groups were formed around a specific problem that had been identified, for example, the need for a playground. Many citizens' groups were organized around demands in the area of housing. One of the best known in the Sixties was the Comité des îlots St-Martin (St. Martin Blocks Committee) in the Little Burgundy neighbourhood of Montréal. Originally, citizens' groups had rather limited goals and operated on a local basis. No attempt was made to find allies outside the neighbourhood, and there was a tendency to refuse to share with other groups. There was a defensive attitude toward "outsiders," which social animators did not do enough to combat.

In the cities, the citizens' groups were the first settings for community work. They were essentially devoted to defending the interests of the residents of a neighbourhood or parish, and were influenced not only by the first professional social animators but also by members of the lower ranks of the clergy, who were sometimes quite militant. One of the best examples of clerical involvement in citizens' groups was Projet d'organisation populaire, d'information et de regroupement (POPIR — People's Organizing and Information Project)[11] in the working-class neighbourhoods of southwest Montréal. Other examples include funding of activities in the south-central area of the city by the Archdiocese of Montréal, the work of Jacques Grand'Maison in St-Jérôme, and Opération dignité groups in the Lower St. Lawrence region.

When we discuss organizations of this kind today, we usually call them popular groups. This change in terminology indicates a change in the perception of the role and objectives of these groups. The question is, whose interests do citizens' groups today defend? The problem with the term "citizens' group" is that it doesn't imply a group of individuals with a common social reality. It suggests a political entity rather than a social or cultural community. Furthermore, with time, the original political impact of the expression has been diluted. To illustrate, let us recall that during the last public sector strike, the moralist Maurice Champagne-Gilbert was the spokesperson for what was described as a "group of eminent citizens," which demanded, among other things, the abolition of the right to strike in health and social service institutions.

Should we conclude, then, that citizens' groups can no longer serve as a basis for organizing? We would suggest that a citizens' group today means a group of individuals mobilized around a particular problem that concerns a whole community — for example, a broad range of people concerned about the pollution of a lake. Rich or poor, all have an interest in the quality of the environment. Such a group is not a popular group, but a citizens' group. Once the problem has been solved to the satisfaction of the majority of the members, the group dissolves. This type of situation offers organizing possibilities for activists and professionals.

Popular groups

The concept of the popular group dates from the early Seventies. It builds on some of the strengths of citizens' groups while breaking with other aspects of them. Among the strengths was the awareness that only collective action can bring about change and that people have a great capacity for mobilization when their interests are threatened. A further result of the experience of the citizens' groups was the questioning of the idea that the working class is the only significant force for change. Citizens' groups had proven the need for power to be in the hands of people representative of their community. And finally, popular education and community organization had gained recognition as the two chief prerequisites for any struggle.

The main break with the citizens' groups was with their localism. Popular groups have developed a much broader vision of action, and their main concerns are problems common to a whole social class. There is much more recognition now of the political nature of these problems and of the need to organize politically to solve them. The need to form alliances with other groups is more and more accepted. As well, professional organizers have seen their leadership strongly contested by new working-class activists. And finally, there has been a spectacular increase in awareness of the oppression of women and the forms it takes in political activism.

The development of popular groups was greatly influenced by the political fervour of the Seventies. First there was FRAP and the infamous events of October 1970. Then there were the political action committees of the post-FRAP period and the emergence of the Marx-ist-Leninist movement, in particular In Struggle and the Workers' Communist Party. On the municipal scene in Québec City and Montréal, political parties were formed by petty-bourgeois elements allied with the popular and union movements. Finally, in 1976, the Parti québécois came to power at the head of a "semi-State," an event that was to have painful consequences for popular groups.

This brief history is intended to emphasize the political importance of popular groups. Not only are they the only arena outside the union movement for large sectors of the population to express themselves; they have also served as a training ground for many politicians. For example, before becoming a star in the Montréal Citizens' Movement and a minister in the first Parti québécois government, Jacques Couture was a community leader in southwest Montréal; Pierre Marois, another Parti québécois minister and at one time seen as a possible successor to Réné Lévesque, was director-general of the federation of ACEFs; Jean Doré, the current mayor of Montréal, was involved in the popular movement as an employee of the Ligue des Droits et Libertés (Human Rights and Liberties League), and was then successor to Marois at the head of the ACEFs. All political parties, but particularly those that call themselves social democratic, such as the Parti québécois and the New Democratic Party, try to recruit candidates and organizers from the ranks of popular organizations.

The above examples show that popular groups are a key arena for action and demonstrate their profoundly democratic nature — they never refuse anyone the right to participate in their activities. This commitment to democracy can be used against these groups, since it leaves them open to takeovers and manipulation.

Popular groups can be divided into two broad categories according to their activities. First, there are activist groups that organize around demands. They are usually fighting a specific form of oppression and attach much importance to education. They include groups of welfare recipients, women's groups, associations of the unemployed, and tenants' associations. The second category is made up of groups whose main activity is service, such as food coops, community daycare centres, literacy groups, and the ACEFs. In practice, however, neither category exists in a pure state, and service and struggle are complementary areas in most groups. The ACEFs and community daycare centres are certainly activist groups as well as service organizations. Many groups, by their very nature, are continually in struggle. Welfare recipients, the unemployed, tenants, and women are often in the front lines.

Other types of groups should also be mentioned. These include resource groups such as popular education centres and the Institut canadien d'Education des Adultes (Canadian Association for Adult Education).[12] There is also a whole cultural sector in the popular movement, which consists of artists involved in music, theatre, and literature.

Popular organizations

We feel it is important to make a distinction between popular groups and popular organizations. This distinction is based on our experience, and we will provide a few examples to illustrate it. A popular organization is a structure that supports and coordinates the activities of popular groups that either are independent or come under the central organization. The development of popular organizations marks a new stage in the history of the popular movement. It is a concrete expression of the groups' refusal of localism and represents a new maturity. There was a time in the late Sixties when it was customary for a group of welfare recipients in a particular neighbourhood to show no concern for people from outside their neighbourhood and even to refuse them services. The formation of a coalition of welfare recipients in Little Burgundy was the first step towards the establishment of the ADDS. The Federation of ACEFs, the Front d'action populaire et de réaménagement urbain (FRAPRU — Front for Popular Action on Urban Planning), and the Regroupement des garderies populaires (Federation of Community Daycare Centres) are other examples of this broadening of popular groups.

The value of such organizations is obvious. They broaden struggles and extend them to the whole of Québec. They demarginalize

oppressed people. They create a power base for the popular movement. How much weight would one volunteer popular group have if
it were not represented by a federation? Popular organizations also
enable us to understand both the extent of oppressive situations and
the particular forms they take — for example, the transportation
problems of welfare recipients living in the country and the inability
of their urban counterparts to pay certain taxes.

Joining together in a popular organization permits groups to put
together a more comprehensive set of demands and present a more
authoritative view of the extent of the problem. It is always stimulat-
ing to know that people elsewhere are fighting to defend the same
interests we are. It is also useful to learn from the experience of groups
in other regions. Popular organizations have a multiplier effect on the
impact of popular groups.

The dangers inherent in these organizations should not, however,
be ignored. Factional battles can immobilize groups for extended
periods. Solidarity is essential to popular groups, but inter-group
squabbles can sap their strength. There is also a tendency to centraliza-
tion that can have a destabilizing effect on groups in the long term.
Furthermore, while paid professional organizers are most at home in
the head offices of organizations, activists are not particularly at ease
there. The head office generally represents an organization in dealings
with the State and funding programmes. Those who work there are
the people's equivalent of the technocrats who work for the government. This can have unfortunate consequences if the staff allow
themselves to be seduced by the sense of power they get from their
command of the issues, their special relationship with the powers-
that-be, and their high profile as official spokespersons.

A staff member of an organization must possess the ability to
analyze and synthesize, the capacity to work under pressure, a
profound sense of democracy, a good knowledge of the issues, a
strong capacity for empathy, and political skills that can be developed
only through long experience. The current strong man in China, Deng
Xiao Ping, once said that the important thing for a cat is not what
colour it is but whether it can catch mice, meaning that an individual's

abilities are more important than his or her ideology. Even though we agree on the need for skills, we believe you do need a certain "colour" to work for a popular organization. The Chinese would certainly not let a Rockefeller run their country. Maybe any expert could be a consultant to a popular organization, but a staff person should agree with the members' analysis of the situation and the direction they have set for their struggles.

NOTES

1. A Jesuit priest who was a social animator in the southwest area of Montréal. In 1974 he ran for mayor under the banner of the Montréal Citizens' Movement, receiving thirty-five percent of the vote. In 1976 he was elected to the National Assembly as Member from St. Henri for the Parti québécois and was appointed to the cabinet. Under pressure from the Vatican, Couture gave up politics and left to continue his ministry in Madagascar. He was considered a man of the left.

2. At the convention of the Federation of CLSCs in November 1987, the minister, Thérèse Lavoie-Roux, stated, "It is not the role of the CLSCs to organize support networks or get involved in economic development." Quoted in *La Presse*, 1 Dec. 1987.

3. The Regroupement Autonome des Jeunes (Autonomous Youth Organization) was an organization of students and young workers that denounced the living conditions imposed on persons under the age of thirty, particularly the discrimination against this age group in determining welfare benefits. (Translators' note: In French, *RAJ* is a homonym for rage.)

4. The FCABQ has been in existence for about twelve years. It includes some fifty Centres d'action bénévole locaux (Local Volunteer Centres).

5. A popular Québec writer who created a television series called "La petite patrie," set in the Villeray neighbourhood of Montréal.

6. Translators' note: This area was so named because molasses was a staple food of the residents.

7. The Sommet populaire was a response to the Parti québécois government's creation of summits bringing together interest

groups on a series of broad issues. Popular Summits have also been held as protests against the economic summits of the seven rich industrialized nations, most recently in Toronto in June 1988.

8. Translators' note: A political movement formed in the early Eighties, whose programme includes socialism, feminism, and independence for Québec.

9. The Brunet Commission (March 1987) recommended narrowing the role of CLSCs. The Harnois Commission (October 1987) on mental health services emphasized a community approach to de-institutionalization and advocated a partnership of State and community groups. The Rochon Commission (February 1988) had a broad mandate covering the whole field of health and social services. It recommended a wider role for CLSCs and reaffirmed the importance of a partnership between State and community groups.

10. There are fourteen Social Service Centres that, together, cover all of Québec. Whereas the 162 CLSCs offer front-line services, Social Service Centres provide more specialized social services. They are also responsible for child protection.

11. Translators' note: POPIR is a homonym for *pas pire,* meaning "not bad," a standard response in colloquial Québec French when someone asks how you are.

12. Translators' note: The ICEA is the autonomous Québec counterpart of the Canadian organization of the same name.

II

GETTING TO KNOW THE COMMUNITY

Whether in a small neighbourhood group or in an organization representing the interests of an entire social class, the *raison d'être* of the organizer is to organize. Organizing is a delicate process and it is important to know the principal techniques. Improvisation can be fatal. In Part Two, we will focus on the preparation required for organizing.

First we will deal with research, a crucial stage in the organizing process. The saying "No research, no right to speak!" is attributed to Mao Tse-Tung. We would add that community workers and activists should never attempt to organize without first doing research. The need to know the community, to understand its dynamics, may seem obvious, but experience tells us that this point bears repeating.

Good research equips you to begin the organizing process on a solid footing. It enables you to identify areas of oppression, to choose your battlefronts, to recognize your potential allies and adversaries, to put a face on power and determine the weapons you will need to fight it. Research will help you avoid mistakes and provide valuable clues as to organizing strategies. It is an essential component of community work.

Three

RESEARCH

It is often said that to change reality, you have to know it. Knowledge is absolutely indispensable for any kind of action that aims to transform reality, whether this reality is natural or social. Before undertaking community action, according to Lucille Beaudry, it is essential to identify: a) the causes of the problems; b) the objectives; c) the order in which these objectives should be pursued; d) resources available and potential allies; and e) our adversaries and the means they have to use against us. This, she says, is what "distinguishes good research, and, at the same time, brings activists and researchers together, gets them used to working with each other, and provides them with opportunities to learn from each other."[1]

Beaudry says that too often when we think of research, we think immediately of huge surveys requiring large budgets and a staff of professional researchers. This idea tends to discourage workers and ordinary citizens from pursuing a thorough understanding of their working and living conditions and taking action to improve them. Research should be considered any activity that enables individuals to better understand their everyday social reality, on the job or in the community. Research is pointless if it remains in the hands of the researchers instead of being used to serve the community. It should be used for education, information, and organization.

Beaudry emphasizes the need to integrate three levels of knowledge of social reality: perceptual, theoretical, and practical. Perceptual knowledge relates to our everyday experience. Theoretical knowledge enables us to order and systematize the data gathered through perceptual knowledge. It is also used to discover causes in order to give the data a broader, more universal meaning. For example, certain aspects of a worker's experience are not specific to his or her situation but apply to many other workers. Finally, practical knowledge lets us transform social reality once a problem has been observed and understood. It is the knowledge applied in the struggles of workers and the oppressed strata of society to advance their interests.

François Lamarche has clearly shown how these three levels of knowledge are central to the Marxist concept of knowledge.[2] He points out, for example, that the acquisition of knowledge consists of extracting concepts from concrete reality and relating these concepts according to their internal logic. He gives the concrete example of a community organizer surveying the neighbourhood in which he or she works, noting the location of the big stores, deterioration of housing, poverty, vacant lots where buildings have been demolished, swaths cut to make way for freeways, the proximity of the neighbourhood to downtown, and signs of grass-roots groups or local activists. Back at his or her desk, the organizer classifies these observations according to categories such as the age and size of buildings, their functions, the occupation, income, and education of residents, and the goals and methods of their organizations.

At this stage, the organizer has a superficial knowledge of the neighbourhood. To know it better, the organizer must examine the internal structure of each of the elements observed and determine their logical relationships. The observer goes beyond what may have seemed obvious at first glance. For example, what relation is there between expansion of the business district and progressive deterioration of housing? The organizer can answer this only by examining the relation of business to the construction and ownership of housing. The expansion of business stimulates land speculation, which, in turn, leads to depreciation of the buildings. Sooner or later the housing gives way to commercial space or luxury housing, at the expense of the local population. This sequence of events is not apparent at first. The observations are connected by the principle of maximization of profit from real estate investment. Understanding this connection is the result of theoretical thinking applied to verifiable facts.

If, as is often the case, community organizers are not able to use what they have learned in university, it is perhaps because their knowledge is based on abstract theories only. Theory is important only insofar as it provides a guide for action. Making the connections between theory and practice is essential for community organizers. Community organizing is both practical and intellectual work. Its tools are a theoretical framework and a body of acquired knowledge. Its product is action to set up a service or a working group, to initiate a struggle or a campaign to make the State act in the interests of a community.

The Purpose of Social Research

Before dealing with the actual steps in research, it is worth asking why we do research in the first place. Unfortunately, research in the social sciences is generally carried out without any concern for practical applications. For us, research means taking a second look and examining something again, more attentively, in order to find out more about it, rather than relying on "common sense" and mere observation. Research in the social sciences should broaden our perspectives on problems and solutions by going beyond the limits of common sense. Theory is necessary since research has to struggle constantly against preconceptions, "common sense," and what appears obvious. If we rely too much on observation and the "obvious," we risk participation in "spontaneous sociology." [3]

Françoise Marquart emphasizes the need for social research to be organized around "constructed objects" [4] that have nothing in common with social facts or social problems as they are perceived by the naïve observer. As Jean-Claude Chamboredon notes in a study on juvenile delinquency, sociologists, like other researchers, often decide on the subject of their research as the result of "a complex process of selection." This leads him to speculate about the danger of "analyzing a manufactured product as if it were a raw material" and to point out that there is a considerable risk, if we are not wary of this danger, of "attributing to delinquents as innate and intrinsic qualities properties that originate in their historical production." [5] Social research consists essentially in testing the "obvious," and conceptions of social problems are often only pre-conceptions based on what appears obvious; consequently, it is important to realize that social problems are constructed. From this point of view, social research strives to destroy stereotypes, to uncover facts, and, most importantly, to reveal the relationships among facts.

The Main Stages in the Research Process

Every organizer is at one time or another faced with the task of preparing a research project or study, even if it is only to improve his or her knowledge of the community or to look for funding for a project. Most "experts" agree that the reason many research projects flounder is because they were not well thought out at the start. Before beginning, it is important to outline the principal stages of the project. Almost every research project, big or small, has four essential stages: preparation, collection of data, analysis of results, and write-up. Each stage is equally important. The natural tendency is to skimp on preparation time, but hasty preparation can result in the subsequent stages taking more time. The written report usually includes a definition of the problem, an analysis of the community, a description of the research methodology, and the presentation and interpretation of results. Adjustments can be made in this format depending on the type of project and whether the report is a preliminary or a final report or part of a grant application.

There are many valid approaches to field research. For example, André Nison[6] sees research in social work as a "tactical operation," a sort of "quest," an "encounter," a "dialogue" — in short, an ongoing exchange between someone who is watching and questioning and a reality that continually gives rise to unforeseen questions without providing final answers. Michel Séguier,[7] speaking from long experience with popular groups, points out that too often we rush into research and come to hasty conclusions without having clearly defined what we are looking for or how we can test it.

The following suggestions should be seen as guidelines only. They are not intended to be followed to the letter, since groups, like individuals, have their own personalities, and act and react in countless ways. Experienced organizers are wary of rigid methods. Nevertheless, the repeated problems experienced by both community workers and students justify a review of some basic rules that apply to any kind of research work, such as reporting on a field placement, applying for a grant, or compiling a dossier.

It is important to keep in mind the similarities between the organizing process and the research process. Too often the two have been seen as distinct. Both the organizer and the researcher must analyze a problem situation, establish a theoretical framework, and formulate objectives and hypotheses in order to modify the situation and solve the problem.[8] In social work, research and action are also closely tied, since the stages of study (research and observation of facts), diagnosis (analysis), and treatment (action) are essentially the same.[9] This also applies to community organizing, which usually involves the following stages: study of the community; identification and analysis of problems in terms of the classic questions of what, where, when, why, how; appraisal of the difficulties; planning and carrying out action; and, finally, assessment of the experience.[10]

Preparing for research

It is important to allow sufficient time for determining the goals and the means. This first stage may delay the start of information-gathering, but the time will be well spent if it results in a clearer definition of the problem. It is sometimes necessary to limit your goals in order to be able to follow the work through to the end. In this preliminary stage, you should articulate your objectives, delimit your area of study, and make an inventory of the resources at your disposal. As Lucien Fabre points out, "When you do not know what you are looking for, you do not know what you have found."[11] This first stage therefore involves these questions: what problems are to be studied and why?, with whom?, and how? There should not, however, be too much emphasis on this stage, or, as happens all too often, the project will never get beyond it.

Many writers have offered practical advice, often based on their own experience, on how to ensure the success of a research project. They emphasize that when research is carried out collectively, as is often the case in popular groups, the team must decide on the work schedule and the distribution of tasks. Group research work requires scrupulous respect for the schedule and strict discipline with regard to the compilation and summarizing of reports. André Jacob, writing about the organization of fieldwork for social work students, lists a number of basic principles. In teamwork, it is important that the members of the team have a common interest in the work. In addition, each member should take part in group discussions of the work and contribute regularly to the group. The team should also establish a structured work plan and a realistic timetable. It may be useful for the group to name a coordinator and a secretary. Finally, it important for the team to evaluate its work regularly in terms of both process and content. In individual work it is equally important to establish a work plan and stick to it, and to consult with colleagues and resource persons when problems arise.[12]

The theoretical and methodological foundations of research

It is important, first, to define the problem or subject to be researched. This step is often the most difficult, and most research projects that go wrong do so at the beginning. The questions asked are either too trivial or too broad, the area of research is poorly defined or inaccessible, or the methods chosen are not appropriate to the problem. It is easy to waste months of hard work on a poorly planned project before the problems become evident. To prevent this, researchers should put considerable thought into formulating the problem. At the same time, however, as Jean-Pierre Deslauriers points out, it is normal for the subject of the research to be rather vague at the beginning, and it is not essential to target it with absolute precision. You must have a good idea of what to do and how to do it, but there should always be room to change course:

Once the researcher knows pretty much where he or she is going, the research can begin. Very often the novice researcher chooses a very broad topic for fear of not having enough material. Sometimes it turns out that the question that has been set is too narrow and must be broadened along the way. But more often the subject chosen is much too broad and must be restricted. It has always seemed to me much easier to reduce the scope of a research project than to broaden it.[13]

This stage often requires a certain amount of bibliographical research. Few research ideas are original, and similar organizing projects may already have been tried. If we reinvented the wheel every day, we would make no progress at all. It is generally useful to do a brief survey of the literature and define your own project in relation to it. There are, however, many views among community organizers on how best to use bibliographical research and the experience of others. Some are wary of being influenced by others' ideas, feeling that they would be less free to develop hypotheses of their own. It is generally agreed, however, that it is useful to make a brief study of the literature on the subject before rushing headlong into a large-scale project. Similarly, we recommend seeking the advice of competent individuals.

Once the bibliography has been completed, you should clarify the objectives. From the beginning you need a clear idea of what results you wish to achieve. It is not enough to say you want to get the facts and then see what needs to be done, because there is a danger of putting research and action on parallel tracks. Objectives should be clearly defined. Research projects are usually initiated to find a solution to a particular problem. The objectives of the research are related to the problem. A general problem must be reduced to its essential elements, the ones that determine the solution. The same logic applies to an action: the goals and the plan must be defined as clearly and realistically as possible.

Once the general problem has been identified and its main components clearly delineated, the hypotheses can be formulated and the theoretical framework refined. Development of the theoretical framework consists in large part of identifying the main variables that influence the phenomenon being studied, and analyzing their interrelationships and previous explanations of these interrelationships.

This is not, however, simply a matter of summarizing the conclusions of other studies. A critical analysis must be made in order to integrate these elements into a true theoretical whole.

Ideally, the theoretical model would meet the following criteria: relevance, inclusiveness, scope, and usefulness. A theoretical model is relevant and inclusive if it enables you to analyze all the data. The scope of the model refers to the variety of situations to which it can be applied. A model is useful if, at a theoretical level, it lets you give meaning to a large number of facts, and, on a concrete level, it points to solutions to social problems. In general, all projects have a more or less explicit conceptual model, which is revealed in the researcher's perception of the phenomenon being studied or the organizer's justification for his or her action.

On the basis of personal knowledge and previous research, the researcher formulates a hypothesis that he or she wishes to test. Hypotheses are often intuitive, anticipated answers to questions. They are essentially avenues for research or attempts to explain certain facts. It is important to formulate hypotheses before going into the field, because they make for greater precision in the gathering of information. Usually there are several attractive hypotheses at the beginning, and others may come to mind along the way. Testing should be restricted to only some of the hypotheses. State your hypotheses in the form of simple questions that call for precise answers. There is nothing to be ashamed of, however, if the data collected do not correspond to the initial hypotheses; it means only that you must formulate new ones. The formulation of hypotheses lets you proceed logically, providing a continuous thread without which the research would be nothing but an indigestible mass of documents and facts. As the great mathematician Poincaré said, "An accumulation of facts is not a science, any more than an accumulation of stones is a house."[14]

Once the theoretical framework has been established, the method of collecting information should be selected. What is required is a step-by-step description of procedures, an operational definition of the variables, a description of the method of sampling, and a description and explanation of each of the information-gathering tools. At this stage, you should make sure that the techniques used are appropriate to the problem and that the sample, in the case of a statistical study, or the subject chosen, in the case of a qualitative study, are representative of the target population. It is important to make sure that the research as a whole could be repeated by other researchers wishing to confirm or to challenge the conclusions.

With regard to the actual methods used to collect information, the researcher has the choice of several techniques, including interviews, participant observation, and content analysis. We should put aside the notion that empirical research necessarily involves questionnaires, and with it the obsession with quantification as a magic formula for objectivity. Community organizers have a rich supply of qualitative material available to them, and they should use it. Interviews, personal journals, autobiographies, correspondence, and official records, when properly used, can add much to research. Content analysis enables the researcher to study the materials objectively, systematically, and quantitatively, and to interpret them in relation to the objectives of the research. Finally, it is essential to remember that social research techniques are only tools. Behind any research process lies the researcher's conception of the facts. Honesty consists not in denying your subjectivity, but rather in trying to harness it and make use of it in your work.

Once the information has been gathered, it should be analyzed and the results presented completely and comprehensibly. Also include all the information needed to understand the results. This does not mean, however, that all the data should be included in the final report. Choices should be made according to the principal hypotheses of the research. In addition, depending on the nature of the data and the methods used in collecting it (observation, interviews, questionnaires, etc.), either quantitative or qualitative analyses, or a combination of the two types, may be made. Quantitative analysis usually involves answering three distinct but complementary questions: 1) what are the correlations among the different variables? 2) what is the probability that these correlations are coincidental? and 3) with how much certainty can we extrapolate from the sample to the population from which it was taken or to other groups? In order to answer these questions, the researcher studies the results and attempts to correlate all the variables until, to the best of his or her knowledge, the most important relationships are clear. To accomplish this, the researcher uses personal knowledge of the subject, the results of other research, and appropriate statistical methods. In a qualitative study, interpretation depends on the analytic abilities and judgement of the researchers.

Publication and distribution of research reports

There are huge numbers of studies gathering dust on shelves because their authors did not take the trouble to pass on their results. Research work is not complete until there exists at least a brief account of the principal stages and the results of the research. This, in our view, is a matter of ethical responsibility to all those involved in the project. Preparing the research report is not any easier than the preceding stages, since the "thrill of discovery," strong at the beginning, will likely have died down somewhat along the way. At the beginning of the project time should be allocated for writing the report, and you should not wait until the last minute to work on it. Most often the data is analyzed and the report written at the same time.

There are no formal rules for writing research reports, but they should be written in a way that will make them accessible to ordinary readers. Traditionally, research reports have a standard form: 1) introduction of the problem; 2) history of the project; 3) results of previous research; 4) hypotheses; 5) procedures used to collect and analyze the data; 6) detailed presentation of the results; 7) summary and interpretation of the results; and 8) conclusions. Finally, it is the practice to include, either within the report or in an appendix, all the tables and questionnaires, interview protocols and statistical breakdowns — in short, all the material required to assess the results. Since research reports can be voluminous, it is customary to produce an abbreviated version in the form of a brief account or an article for a journal.

Too many reports lie unread on the bookshelves of professors and students. How many times have we heard organizers and activists complain of having been "plundered" for information by all kinds of research projects they never heard from again. Simple courtesy requires that researchers give some consideration to the people from whom they get their information. Too often social research is merely a means of academic advancement. Some think it is enough to publish their work in learned journals. It is certainly legitimate for professional researchers to want to present the results of their work to their colleagues and employers, but these results should also be made available to the general public. Too often, results are presented in such select, scholarly language that the audience is reduced to a small circle of friends and colleagues. To get out of the "academic ghetto," we must learn to express ourselves. Clear and simple language does not detract from the rigour and seriousness of an analysis. Making the results of our efforts available to the people with whom we work is an important task for community organizers.

You should not wait until a study has been completed to make your findings known. Making this an ongoing concern permits a continuing dialogue and a constant process of feedback. There are many ways of publicizing findings — posters, exhibitions, public meetings, audio-visual presentations, films, talks, press releases, cartoons, and theatre. The choice depends in part on the nature of the information to be distributed, the size of the audience you wish to reach, and the time and resources available. The requirement that results be published can be an advantage to a research team since it forces them to respect deadlines and draw provisional conclusions. Without this discipline, they can get caught up in the complexities of the project and never obtain any useful results.

It is generally recognized, however, that reporting the results of research to the people concerned does not necessarily lead to outpourings of joy and expressions of eternal gratitude. Returning results to sources can be a delicate process, and it is not often done. The research findings can provoke a kind of crisis within the group studied, and this reaction carries over into the relationship with those presenting the findings. Yet a study can also stimulate real dialogue among the members of a group, and reporting your results to your subjects can be exciting for an organizer. As well as providing a learning experience, it can demonstrate to organizers that they actually serve a useful purpose, which is no small accomplishment these days.

Research Techniques

Participant observation

Analysis of a community is often associated with participant observation, in which the researcher, instead of using so-called "objective" methods such as surveys, becomes directly involved in the life of the community in order to understand significant attitudes and behaviours from within. Contrary to what some may believe, participant observation is actually a systematic approach with a pre-established research plan based on the goals of the investigation.

Caplow, Fortin[15] and others have proposed the following basic guidelines for participant observation:

> *a) Participant observation is used mainly with small groups or communities, and provides qualitative information.*
> *b) The observer must be accepted by the group or community (which limits the use of this method, because some groups reject it outright).*
> *c) As far as possible, the observer should try not to influence the functioning of the group or community.*
> *d) Like any other technique, participant observation should be used in conjunction with additional methods, such as interviews or historical or documentary research.*

There are a number of issues involved in participant observation. Some consider that concealment is necessary to enable researchers to integrate into the group or community, arguing that, otherwise, they remain outsiders, thus modifying the situation being observed. There is always a risk that the observer will remain outside the group's significant experience or, on the other hand, be completely absorbed by it: this is a constant dilemma for the participant observer. Observations may become distorted over time, because participant observation demands time and emotional presence on the part of the researcher. Finally, there is the question of how much information the participant observer should have beforehand. Pre-conceived ideas may prejudice the researcher's observations, but naïveté can be equally harmful.

Preliminary information on the group's history, methods, and values is often necessary.

As for the problem of gaining entry to the group, there are rare occasions when this comes almost naturally, with the personal qualities of the observer, shared ethnic background or neighbourhood, or the presence of friends in the group facilitating the researcher's acceptance. In most cases, however, researchers must use more indirect methods. Some may learn new job skills and get themselves hired, while others may even convert to a new religion. Should such tactics prove impractical, some researchers may resort to using informers instead of participant observers; this is a tactic best left to the police.

The researcher may use a variety of methods, including interviews and questionnaires. However, these methods can only contribute to the research if they involve comprehensive observation. This is not just a matter of seeing and hearing, nor of using high-quality audio-visual equipment. Most important of all, the observation should never be divorced from the context, which gives it its meaning.

Action research

Action research makes it possible to construct a model while at the same time providing opportunities for collaboration between researchers and community workers. The literature describes action research in the following terms:

a) Everyone involved in the group being studied takes part in the action research process. The subject-object relationship between researchers and group is eliminated and the research is carried out by all, for all.
b) The basis of action research is a concrete experience involving both analysis and organizing.
c) The choice of the problems focused on is based on socially recognized needs rather than the researchers' personal or professional interests.
d) For maximum effectiveness, action research is often multi-disciplinary.
e) Normally carried out on a restricted scale, the action research project is often designed in such a way as to provide generalizable conclusions regarding social change.

f) Researchers work not with artificially created groups made up of isolated individuals, but with real groups rooted in their usual context of life and work.

g) Action research requires involvement, evaluation, and self-analysis over time, and cannot be reduced to a few isolated actions.

h) Action research should provide new knowledge, both on the particular questions being researched and on the researchers themselves insofar as they are objects of the research.

i) Researchers should not place themselves in a neutral or external position in relation to the group; their attitude should be that of a participant, ranging from empathy to active involvement.

j) Since the researchers are personally and socially involved in action research, they may find themselves questioning their personal and family history, their class positions, and their political beliefs.

k) Action research aims to develop more effective organizing methods by providing a better understanding of the dynamics of group action and through the ongoing evaluation of results. It may use traditional research methods, both quantitative and qualitative.

Paul de Bruyne provides an interesting definition of action research: *Action research aims to know and to act at the same time. It is a kind of dialectic of knowledge and action. Instead of confining itself to using existing knowledge, as applied research does, it creates changes in a natural situation and then analyses the conditions and results of these changes.*[16]

Action research is not merely a method or procedure; above all, it is a reflection of a particular understanding of the process of gaining knowledge.

The action research approach is an appealing one because it symbolically (some would even say magically) connects ideas that social research practice has usually kept separate: theory and practice, research and action, the psychological and the social, individual and collective, emotional and intellectual. However, many authors[17] have expressed reservations about the validity of action research. Our own interest in this method does not imply that we support it unconditionally or consider it a panacea. On the contrary, as we have shown, we are aware of both its strengths and its limitations.

"Activist" research

Research on popular groups differs slightly from other types of action research. Popular groups usually have their own researchers, animators, and natural leaders, although, often, these individuals are not able to make themselves heard in today's society.[18] They also have their own organizing principles and ways of operating. Too rigid a formal structure could hinder a group rather than help it. Nevertheless, a minimum of organization is necessary from the very beginning.

A working group should be formed and the research priorities established collectively. The process should be delayed until some degree of consensus is reached; failure to do so will only result in constant questioning of the objectives set and the results achieved. Different experiences have used a variety of methods, but one common denominator always emerges: the importance of forming an initial core group. In the preparatory phase, those who will be working together must become acquainted and agree on consultation and decision-making procedures. The broadest possible consensus should be aimed for, while respecting individual personalities and abilities and allowing the freedom needed for research.

The first meetings are often difficult because of the large number of problems to be solved and the need to analyse the situation and identify the possibilities for action. Despite these uncertainties, consensus and solidarity can develop and grow. The group may wish, at first, to remain free of institutional or political ties, and allow links with official authorities, organizations, and the general public to develop progressively. Whatever choices are made, hasty decisions and endless discussions should both be avoided. The members of the group should have a good grasp of the historical background of their situation and its present-day effects. The largest possible number of people should be involved in both planning and carrying out the research. But doesn't this prolong the process needlessly, discouraging participation and taking energy away from more urgent matters? The experience of

popular groups in Québec shows that it often results in greater awareness and increased participation. Developing an ability for research and
systematic observation can clearly help a group organize more effectively.

Activist research is politically and ideologically committed. As
Yves Vaillancourt[19] has stated, it is a form of action research in which
the researchers unite with the working classes in order to effect social
change and abolish exploitative and oppressive relationships. The
hallmark of this method is its stance in favour of trade unions and
popular groups. Many researchers have noted an increasing trend in
the social sciences toward the study of oppressed groups, particularly
those involved in struggles for power. This raises the issue of the
political stakes involved in research as well as that of the researcher's
role. Researchers should guard against the results of their investigations
being used by those in power to strengthen their domination and
control.

Sometimes activist research in the service of the working classes
is confused with an approach in which researchers confine themselves
to studying the working classes, using only data gathered in this milieu.
There are quite a number of experts living—very comfortably —on
"poverty studies." Research that contributes to the progress of working
class struggles also has to study "the enemy camp." Activist researchers, while remaining conscious of the limitations of official information, should try to arm themselves with ammunition supplied by
governments and employers.

Various authors[20] have suggested guidelines for activist research
that is relevant and effective. It must be fed directly by questions raised
in action, and, in turn, the knowledge it produces must serve as a tool
for change. Without this constant, immediate, and organic relationship
between theory and practice, research produces nothing but more
books for university bookshelves. A growing number of researchers are
recognizing that research in itself has no meaning, and are seeking to
make their work personally and socially meaningful. Doing so means
establishing organic links with activists and organizations directly
involved in struggle.

It is important to remember, however, that the researcher's contribution to the struggle is to carry out research. Researchers have to be able not only to participate in the group's activities without feeling guilty for taking time away from their research, but also to carry out their research without feeling guilty for not being in the front lines of the struggle. This conflict is common among activist researchers involved in community groups. In our view, it can be resolved by a clear distribution of tasks and an understanding of the constraints inherent in activist research. It is important that activist researchers prove their skills; otherwise they will only increase working-class mistrust of "intellectuals" and confirm the view that activists are incapable of doing "real" research.

Freire's Conscientization[21] *Approach*

This approach has the following characteristics:

> *a) Instead of merely getting the population to take part in their research, the researchers participate not as "experts" but as resource persons, in research initiated by popular groups.*
> *b) The results are provided not only to the sponsors of the project or to the "initiated," but to the entire target population.*
> *c) Research starts from the action of a group and aims to shed light on that action.*

In this type of research, the hypotheses for research are also hypotheses for action. The group maintains decision-making power over the orientations of the research. The aims are the following:

> *a) The means and methods used should be able to be mastered by groups of ordinary people.*
> *b) The research process should be controlled by the group involved.*
> *c) The research process itself should be one of conscientization.*
> *d) The research should lead to action.*

An approach of this kind has been developed by the collective La maitresse d'école (The Schoolteacher). This group of progressive teachers sees the research project as "a concrete task defined and carried out by a group, which mobilizes the group because it is the expression of a collective will, and leads to concrete, material, communicable, useful results."[22] Freire has emphasized the need for organizers to understand the cultural reality of the people with whom they work. His ideas have been influential in francophone popular education and social work circles, largely through the work of the Ecumenical Institute for the Development of Peoples (INODEP), particularly that of Humbert. Freire shows how the political domination of education silences the oppressed. He contrasts liberating education with "banking education," in which one gives, the other receives, one thinks, the other "is thought," and being educated means receiving, retaining, and repeating knowledge. "Banking education" is domesticating; its aim is to control people's lives and actions by encouraging them to adjust to the world. It inhibits creativity and the power to act. Liberating education, on the other hand, emphasizes the capacity of individuals and groups to be creators of culture and subjects of history. It aims to teach people not only to read and write but also to analyse and transform their environment.

Freire's approach has influenced literacy and popular education projects on five continents, among them some in Québec.[23] The Collectif québécois de pratiques de conscientisation (Québec Collective on Conscientization Techniques)[24] describes a number of these projects, including that of the Organisation pour les droits sociaux? Mercier (Mercier Organization for Social Rights), which has been organizing "cultural circles" since 1979. The aim of these groups, which are made up of about twenty welfare recipients, is to help the members break out of their isolation, increase their feelings of self-worth, break down prejudices, become aware of their rights, and build solidarity. The animators of the groups adapted Freire's literacy method for use in their conscientization sessions. Their experience confirms that, in a class society, the oppressed class develops individual and collective mechanisms of self-deprecation, feelings of helplessness, incompetence, and inferiority, as a result of social and economic exploitation. These feelings discourage them from fighting for their rights. Given this situation, Freire's approach is necessary and useful.

"Sociological Intervention"?

Alain Touraine is one of the French sociologists whose work has been very influential in Québec, particularly among the current generation of organizers. He developed his method of analysis of social relations through his interest in studying social movements. Since social relationships are not immediately apparent, the purpose of "sociological intervention" is to bring them out and clarify their underlying meaning. This approach, which has thus far been used only with protest groups, involves creating a give-and-take relationship between researchers and activists, and between analysis and action. The demand for the research should come from the activists. The research is organized in terms of a knowledge objective, the aim being to understand how collective action arises and social movements are built. The more deeply committed the researchers are, the more they will learn about the formative processes of their own action. The goal of sociological intervention is to understand society as it is being formed, by studying the opposition movements that shape it.

The method involves the formation of a group of about twenty activists representing different tendencies or organizations within the same movement, such as the anti-nuclear movement, the nationalist movement, or the student movement. These people take part in the process as individuals, and not as spokespersons for their groups. The researchers initiate a process of group self-analysis in order to clarify the goals of the struggle or conflict in which the activists are involved and to increase their "capacity for historic action." The researchers play a dual role: as animators and agitators strengthening the group, and as recorders, serving as the group's memory and maintaining a certain critical distance. Sociological intervention takes place with two different groups simultaneously. The groups meet in order to better understand the implications of their actions and the conflicts they experience. Discussion takes place not only among the participants but also with their opponents.

Sociological intervention is an innovative approach less because of its subject matter — the study of social conflict — than because of its method of working with small groups. It avoids focusing on the group itself, its interpersonal relations or group psychology, and instead introduces confrontation with individuals from outside the group, chosen from among its allies or opponents. The researchers adopt the point of view of the social movement they are studying. But the researchers are not part-time activists, nor are the activists junior research associates. Even when they are involved in analysing their actions, the activists remain activists; the focus on action is never absent, and the group never becomes a mere discussion group. The researchers centre on the history of the group, making hypotheses as to the conditions and possibilities of its development or transformation into a true social movement.[25]

Hamel and Léonard have identified four conditions for sociological intervention[26].

> a) *The researchers should form a relationship with the social movement and the activists must agree to take part in the research.*
> b) *The group must go beyond the ideological level to focus on actions and strategies. In order to do so, the group is confronted with a series of individuals ranging from its own grass-roots supporters to opponents.*
> c) *The role of the researcher is to bring out the issue in conflict; this role becomes more important as the group process draws to a close.*
> d) *The process of analysis should be considered part of the group's action. It is on an equal footing with action, for a time replacing the concrete goals of action. The group's work of self-analysis also constitutes the research.*

Dubert and Wievorka have questioned the value of sociological intervention.[27] Considering that it aims for a knowledge objective — understanding of the processes by which collective actions arise and social movements are built — they suggest that while it may satisfy researchers, it has less to offer activists. It seems to us, however, that it answers the constant need of activists to understand the meaning of their actions and that, by revealing the formative processes of their action, it can help them bridge the gap between their theoretical positions and the practices they develop. Far from discouraging or weakening activists, it can only increase their ability to act.

NOTES

1. Lucille Beaudry,*Guide de recherche à l'intention des militants* (Montréal: Centre coopératif de recherches en politique sociale, 1975), p. 7. (Translators' note: This is a free translation.)

2. François Lamarche, *Une Ville à vendre (Cahier 1: Pour une analyse marxiste de la question urbaine)* (Québec: Conseil des Oeuvres de Québec, 1972), pp. 17-19.

3. Pierre Bourdieu, Jean-Claude Chamboredon, and Jean-Claude Passeron, *Le Métier de sociologue* (Paris: Mouton/Bordas, 1968), p. 430.

4. "La recherche peut-elle être sociale," *Informations sociales*, No. 7 (July 1973), p. 31.

5. "La délinquance juvénile, essai de construction d'objet" in *Revue française de sociologie*, Vol. 12 (1971), pp. 335-77. (Translators' note: This is a free translation.)

6. "Propositions méthodologiques" in *Travail social et Méthodes d'enquête sociologique* (Paris: Les Editions ESF, 1975), p. 51.

7. *Critique institutionnelle et Créativité collective* (Paris: Editions L'Harmattan, 1976), p. 148.

8. Jacques Rhéaume, "La recherche-action: un nouveau mode de savoir?" in *Sociologie et Sociétés*, Vol. 14, No. 1 (1982), p. 44.

9. Francine Ouellet-Dubé, "Recherche ou pratique: qui gagne?" in *Service social*, Vol. 28, Nos. 2-3 (1979), p. 6.

10. Marie-Hélène de Bousquet, *Le Service social* (Paris: Presses Universitaires de France, collection Que sais-je, No. 1173, 1965), p. 68.

11. Quoted in Henri Desroches, *Apprentissage en sciences sociales et éducation permanente* (Paris: Editions Ouvrières, 1971), p. 51. (Translators' note: This is a free translation.)

12. *Guide méthodologique pour la recherche et l'action sociale* (Montréal: Nouvelles Frontières, 1984), p. 9.

13. "Guide de recherche qualitative" in *Bulletin de recherche*, No. 62 (1982), p. 2. (Translators' note: This is a free translation.)

14. *La Science et l'hypothèse*, Chapter 9. (Translators' note: This is a free translation.)

15. T. Caplow, *L'Enquête sociologique* (Paris: A. Colin, 1970), pp. 149-63; and A. Fortin, "L'observation participante: au coeur de l'altérité" in J.-P. Deslauriers, ed., *Les méthodes de la recherche qualitative* (Québec: Presses de l'Université du Québec, 1987), pp. 23-24.

16. Paul de Bruyne, et al., *Dynamique de la recherche en sciences sociales* (Paris: Presses Universitaires de France, 1974), p. 110. (Translators' note: This is a free translation.)

17. For example, Ricardo Zuniga, "La recherche-action et le contrôle du savoir" in *Revue internationale d'action communautaire* (Montréal), Vol. 5, No. 45 (Spring 1981), pp. 35-45; and P. Dominicé, "L'ambiguïté des universitaires face à la recherche-action," pp. 51-58.

18. J. Grand'Maison, *Vers un nouveau savoir* (Montréal: HMH, 1969), p. 72.

19. Yves Vaillancourt, "Quelques difficultés rencontrées dans la recherche militante" in *Actes du colloque sur la recherche-action* (Université du Québec à Chicoutimi) (October 1981), pp. 62-72.

20. *Ibid.*; P.Y. Troutot, "Sociologie d'intervention et recherche-action socio-politique" in *Revue Suisse de sociologie*, No. 6 (1980), pp. 191-206; and D. Fortin, "La recherche-action à caractère militant: le cas du GRAP" in *Service social*, Vol. 36, Nos. 2-3 (1985), pp. 269-91.

21. Translators' note: Freire has defined conscientization as "the process in which men, not as recipients, but as knowing sub-

jects, achieve a deepening awareness both of the sociocultural reality that shapes their lives and of their capacity to transform that reality," in "Cultural Action and Conscientization" in *The Politics of Education: Culture, Power and Liberation*, trans. Donaldo Macedo (South Hadley, Mass.: Bergin and Garvey, 1985), no. 2, p. 93.

22. Paulo Freire, *La Pédagogie des opprimés* (Paris: Maspero, 1974).
23. M. Ouellette, "Pédagogie militante" in *Revue internationale d'action communautaire*, Vol. 3, No. 43 (1981), pp. 101-11; P.P. Hautecoeur, "Le point sur l'alphabétisation au Québec" in *Revue internationale d'action communautaire*, Vol. 3, No. 43 (1981), pp. 111-27; and S. Wagner and M. Lapierrière, "L'alphabétisation à Pointe St-Charles, pp. 127-45.

24. G. Ampleman, et al., *Pratiques de conscientisation, expériences d'éducation populaire au Québec* (Montréal: Nouvelle Optique, 1983), and *Pratiques de conscientisation 2* (Collectif québécois d'édition populaire, 1987).

25. Alain Touraine, *La Voix et le Regard*, p. 200.

26. P. Hamel and J.-F. Léonard, *Les Organisations populaires, l'Etat et la Démocratie* (Montréal: Nouvelle Optique, 1981).

27. F. Dubert and M. Wievorka, "L'intervention sociologique" in *Revue internationale d'action communautaire*, Vol. 5, No. 45 (1981), pp. 115-22.

Four

UNDERSTANDING THE COMMUNITY

Individuals and groups are asking for tools to help them analyze the communities in which they work. There is plenty of basic information available, particularly quantitative data on incomes, industries, housing, etc., but all too often people don't know what to do with it. It is important to know how to select and analyze information in order to use it effectively in community work. Another basic problem every community organizer faces is understanding the major changes that have taken place in recent years in society and in the nature of social action itself.

The first part of this chapter will discuss the relevance of the concept of community. We will then attempt to identify basic aspects of a community with which organizers should be familiar in order to understand it fully. Thirdly, we will briefly contrast two concepts of community: the medical concept and the social concept. We will conclude the chapter by discussing the meaning of community in present-day society.

The Community

Organizers always work in a community, that is, with a group of individuals who share a physical space and a number of common interests. The activities of groups involved in community organizing do not concern their members alone. The entire community is addressed and called upon to take part, therefore it should be seen not as a passive spectator but as an actor. The success of any organizing effort depends on the response of the community. That is why understanding the community is essential for the organizer.[1]

Many writers have suggested that industrialization, urbanization, bureaucratization, and "massification" — the development of mass society — have contributed to a significant weakening of the local community. While we do not deny the relevance of these analyses, it seems clear to us that community organizing can be carried out only on the basis of an identified community living in a defined territory. A local community has a culture that, while sharing much with neighbouring communities, is distinct in many ways. It seems obvious, for example, that a rural community is different from an urban working-class neighbourhood, and that a community with a tourist-based economy is very different from one that depends on heavy industry. This is why we feel that the concept of the local community has lost none of its importance. We do admit, however, that with time local communities undergo changes, sometimes major ones.[2]

Most writers agree that the local community has not disappeared, but rather changed in nature to become more of a collectivity. This is the view of Roland L. Warren, who distinguishes between two basic models of the community: the vertical model, in which links with systems outside the community are predominant, and the horizontal model, in which structural and functional relations within the community predominate.[3] This distinction enables us to focus on an important phenomenon in modern society, namely the strengthening of the vertical and the weakening of the horizontal aspects of the community. It also allows us to explain the development of community work as essentially an attempt to strengthen the horizontal aspects of the community. In other words, Warren approaches the community as a social system made up of both internal and external forces. The internal forces arise from interrelations among members of the community, and the external forces arise from outside the community. The development of the State has involved an increase in the influence of the external forces and what appears to be a weakening of the fabric of the community.

This might be more accurately viewed as a transformation of the community.

Marcel Rioux has described Québec as a "closely knit" society, referring to the longstanding importance of social ties.[4] Without idealizing the past, we can say that in Québec, as elsewhere, industrialization and urbanization have upset the old forms of social solidarity. We have already mentioned the negative consequences of "urban renewal" projects in the working-class neighbourhoods of Québec's major cities. In the name of "slum clearance," the homes of thousands of working-class families have been destroyed and the most defenceless — the elderly, the unemployed, welfare recipients, single-parent families — have been "ghettoized" in public housing. In addition, many of the factories, churches, schools, movie theatres, and recreational facilities that were traditionally part of these neighbourhoods have disappeared. This process of change has destroyed the integrity and solidarity that bound private life, social life, and working life in these communities. With the breakdown of the traditional social fabric, individuals now often find themselves completely alone or with only their family networks to turn to.[5]

Even the family unit has not been spared. It has been completely transformed, as the dramatic rise in the numbers of divorces and single-parent families shows. These changes have had an effect on social solidarity, particularly with regard to children and the elderly. In the case of the elderly, most Québec workers experience a reduction in their standard of living and their social circle when they retire.

The experience of social workers in the cities tells us a great deal about the role of external forces in the changes that have taken place in local communities. Jérôme Guay has found that although urban renewal has substantially changed the makeup of many neighbourhoods, it has not destroyed the local community. There is a greater variety of occupational groups, the extended family is more dispersed geographically, and people with the same interests and needs tend to unite in organizations. It is in these organizations, according to Guay, rather than in their geographical place of residence, that people find a feeling of belonging and personal identity. Sports clubs, professional associations, and self-help groups have now replaced the community life that once existed in the neighbourhood.

More fundamentally, Guay points out, there has been a major change in the power structure, and the neighbourhood is no longer a centre of decision-making. For example, small corner grocers now belong to national chains that make many decisions for them, neighbourhood schools receive their directives from the ministry of education, and similar comments can be made regarding the City Council, the Chamber of Commerce, and the Caisse Populaire (parish credit union), leading Guay to conclude that the neighbourhood has been stripped of its power.[6] Most other studies show that the urban community persists despite these changes but that it now takes varied forms. Social cohesion and solidarity have not completely disappeared, but they come to the fore only when there is a danger or when a common problem requires neighbours to help each other.

There is also an increasing tendency today to look at community organizing from a less local point of view. Thus, the Association pour la défense des droits sociaux (ADDS — Association for the Defence of Social Rights), the Mouvement Action-Chômage (Unemployment Action Movement), and many other organizations have taken a broad approach to the problems with which they deal, considering them from the point of view of the whole social group concerned. While it is desirable to go beyond local concerns, however, community workers still have to work in a specific area and with the human community of that area. How, then, should they go about gaining a better understanding of that community?

Aspects of the Community

In his classic text on social animation in an urban setting, Michel Blondin provides a clear picture of the type of information necessary for community work, identifying five main categories: 1) statistical information on the general structure of the community; 2) an inventory of existing community resources in the neighbourhood; 3) information on the power networks and social networks in the neighbourhood; 4) information on the community's values (necessary though often difficult to obtain); and 5) residents' perceptions of social problems and needs.[7]

Demographics

First, it is important to be familiar with statistical data on the community, such as demographic and socioeconomic information, including ethnic origins and language, in order to know its general characteristics and to compare it with other neighbourhoods. It is essential to know the characteristics of the people living in the neighbourhood. Are they elderly? Young couples? Roomers living alone? What is the population density? The rate of births and deaths? How many people are unemployed and living on welfare? What is the average income? What are the crime statistics? The rate of hospitalization?

This demographic information should be placed in a historical context, hence it is important to know the history of the neighbourhood. Many groups have done work on the history of their communities. A slide show on the history of housing in Montréal, produced by the Service d'aménagement populaire (Popular Urban Planning Service) in 1979, is a good example.

Statistical information today is an essential tool in any critique of social reality. For it to be useful and relevant, however, choices must be made and relationships found among various data. For example, we better understand the historical evolution of certain urban neighbourhoods in Québec when we realize that the deterioration of housing is always accompanied by major changes in industrial structure, demographics, and land use in these neighbourhoods.

Inventory of resources

Once the community has been described, you must determine who is providing the services. Making this inventory will let you complete your picture of the community, evaluate what forces can be mobilized, and establish contact with representatives of the various organizations and lay the groundwork for cooperation.

Many organizations have published inventories of community resources in the form of lists or directories, and some enjoy a fairly wide distribution. Although they are essentially descriptive, these publications can be an excellent way in which to get to know the community, since they enable organizers to go beyond the small circles of people with whom they have professional or ideological affinities to develop a more objective notion of what resources the community has to offer.

Understanding power networks and social networks

Community organizers, as many writers have emphasized, have often held a mythical view of the community as a homogeneous world united in solidarity, disregarding the real relations of power and property.[8] Organizers must be aware of the local power elite, the owners of the factories, the businesses, the housing, and the land, and those who hold political power at the federal, provincial, and municipal levels. Community organizations, church groups, social clubs, school committees, Caisses Populaires (parish credit unions), recreation groups, merchants' associations, and ethnic associations are also part of the formal and informal structures of local power, and should be studied carefully.

Community organizers should take as much interest in people's working conditions as in their living conditions. Although there is an abundance of data, it takes firsthand research to understand the real conditions. This presents other problems, however, such as how to get access to factories. Most large businesses now have public relations personnel, who will usually welcome researchers — until the questions get too complicated or too sensitive. The researcher must be tactful and have a prepared questionnaire.

Power is important in relations between the organizer and the population. Organizers should abandon the myth of the superiority of professional knowledge and accept the people as active partners in their process of learning about the community. This brings us to the social networks in which the real "people's experts" are to be found. The circle of friends and family members with whom people share personal problems is relatively small, especially in an urban setting. In addition to these close ties, there are acquaintances they see regularly but with whom they are less intimate, and who provide access to a more varied world. The individual enlarges his or her social network by participating in the context of the neighbourhood, school, work, and organizations. This social network provides not only emotional support, but also socialization, recreation, and exchange of services. It is important that the organizer be familiar with these networks.

Guy Paiement suggests making a map of one's own social networks, identifying the people with whom one is in regular contact:

> ...these persons live somewhere, in a specific neighbourhood. They belong to a particular community and social class. We take note of this. They buy clothing and food according to specific tastes. They share with us certain recreational activities, books, and newspapers. When we meet, they are concerned about their children, their jobs or their lack of jobs, their debts, their future. As much as possible, we take note of what we observe, and little by little, the map of our everyday relationships emerges, which will likely also be the map of our shared assumptions, our social aspirations, our cultural prejudices, our solidarities, and our hopes. I think that almost anyone can draw their own map... Maybe then we will know if we are dreaming our lives or living our dreams of justice and sharing.[9]

Understanding values

Organizers have often been criticized for not making enough effort to understand the people with whom they work. To reach the people of a community, it is important to understand their values, keeping in mind that a community's values are not necessarily homogeneous and often vary according to social class. This understanding does not come easily: it requires patience, observation, and a certain amount of empathy and intuition.

The best way to learn about people's experience and culture is through observation and discussion. Just by driving or walking through the neighbourhood, you can gain information about housing conditions, ethnic makeup, and meeting places such as bars and restaurants. All this should be noted and perhaps recorded on a map. Being present enables the organizer to put a finger on the pulse of the neighbourhood and to obtain otherwise inaccessible information. In addition, the organizer's visibility in the community outside working hours promotes acceptance by the population. Organizers should get involved in the life of the neighbourhood by talking to residents on the street and in organizations, spending time in bars, shopping in local stores, and attending local celebrations and City Council meetings. They can thus identify those people who should be interviewed at length.

Informants should be representative of the neighbourhood and know it well. Clergy, teachers, visiting nurses, members of social and recreational clubs, and even barbers and barmaids have extensive contact with the community and should be interviewed. Key informants should not be limited to professional or institutional interviewees. Ordinary citizens, such as the elderly, volunteer workers, and people considered marginal or deviant, should be included. We are speaking here of informal discussions rather than any kind of systematic survey or questionnaire. Once the organizer has an idea of the perceptions of the people in the neighbourhood, the next two major areas to explore are needs and problems, and possible solutions.

Analysis of needs and problems

"Need analysis" is a catchall term, one that allows us to justify practically anything and to conceal our own economic, political, and professional interests. A social need is experienced by people and is consequently marked by their subjectivity. The determination of social needs has always been a two-fold process, with individuals, or more often groups, claiming needs and even rights, with other individuals and groups opposing their claims.[10] Like it or not, that is how the world operates. Despite the good faith of organizers and researchers, the analysis of a community's needs often amounts to a negation of that community. This occurs when researchers project onto a population "needs" that the people themselves have not expressed. Then social workers act as if the community had requested the solutions they have proposed: social services, cultural animation, etc. The needs that are identified are the needs of those who define the problems, and in this way some people's problems become other people's needs.[11]

Professionalism in social services has been criticized as dehumanizing. Professionals define needs essentially as deficiencies, and this results almost automatically in fragmenting people and individualizing and psychologizing their problems. Stated in personal terms, the ideology of professionalism claims three things: 1) that you are deficient; 2) that you are the problem; 3) that you have many problems. From the perspective of professional, corporatist, and trade-union interests, these postulates become: 4) we need problems; 5) we need to tell you what your problems are; and, finally, 6) we are the answer to your problems. The ideology of professionalism is a worldview in which life and society are treated as a series of technical problems, turning citizens into clients and communities into conglomerations of deficient individuals.[12] This vision of the world dehumanizes the consumers of services, denying them any say in either the definition or the solution of their problems.

To counter this ideology, conditions must be created that enable the people concerned to truly express their own needs. By "needs," we mean the formulation of specific problems and the conditions that cause them. For people to really express their needs, they must not be artificially separated from the community in which they live, because their everyday living conditions are an integral part of the definition of the problem. Therefore, it is essential to go into the community to fully understand its problems. People must also be brought together in order to break down the isolation of individuals and permit the collective expression of needs rather than purely individual views.[13]

Approaches to the Community

There are two main ways of approaching a community and its needs: the objective or macro-social approach, and the subjective or micro-social approach. The macro-social approach involves the use of extensive surveys, while the micro-social approach usually focuses on the various networks that exist in a community. The two approaches are complementary, however, and, as much as possible, should be used together. To give a concrete example, community health programmes in Québec are pulled between two opposing concepts of community, a medical concept and a social concept. In terms of impact, the first concept clearly appears to predominate. These two perspectives give rise to very different approaches to providing services.[14]

The medical concept

Epidemiology's goal of understanding the distribution of health problems in the population leads it to split the community into sub-groups that are as specific as possible. Consequently, the predominant approach to providing services is through "programmes" aimed at "target populations" that are homogeneous with regard to age, sex, place of work, level of education, etc. Like the medical specialist's patient, the community is not considered in its totality, as a complete and complex entity. This medical approach also tends to professional-ize the relationship with the community: we are the professionals who know the health needs of this population; we are therefore going to offer the services we consider appropriate; of course, we are in favour of participation, but only on our terms.

The social concept

This approach, which has roots in anthropology and sociology and in social work, sees a community as more than an aggregate of persons who happen to live within the same territory, more than a bunch of target-populations receiving various services. In this view, a community is a relatively structured entity with its own dynamics, an entity whose people share a culture and an awareness of belonging. The social perspective stresses the need to understand the dynamics of the specific community. It also encourages us to see the community as a totality, to study its natural groups, and to act on the basis of the perceptions of the people rather than those of the professionals.

Instead of continuing to place these perspectives in opposition, we can try to use them together in such a way that they complement one another, combining their strengths, the statistical methods and efficient use of resources of the medical approach, and the sensitivity to the community's complexity and the capacity to see action in a broader context that mark the social approach. The only way to bring about effective and lasting change is to directly involve the community and act according to its perceptions, its capacity to accept change, and its priorities.

Relations with the Community

Community organizers must know themselves; they must have a clear perception of their strengths and weaknesses and their personal and professional motivations.[15] Start by taking a close look at yourself as an individual and try to measure your personal resources, interests, and aptitudes. This process of self-knowledge also involves maintaining a self-critical approach to professional attitudes, allowing them to be challenged by the realities of the work. For whom and with whom are we working? In whose interest? Who or what are we defending? These are the fundamental questions we must ask ourselves. The following attitudes have been shown to be essential for the successful organizer.

Know why you are there and be open and honest about it

This means setting personal objectives that are clear and concrete. These objectives serve as a guide in your research and determine how you present yourself to the community. In all your dealings, you must be sincere and comfortable with the image you project, and not "play" at being what you are not. You must be clear about your status.

Respect cultural differences

It might be desirable for organizers to work only in their own communities or in communities like them, but this is not always possible. We must therefore assume that there will be major cultural differences between organizers and the working-class communities with whom they work. While this is not a very comfortable situation at the beginning, alliances between organizers and working-class communities are possible as long as each party respects the other. Embracing "workerism" is not the solution. The key to success is building a relationship in which academic learning and everyday experience complement one another in the pursuit of shared objectives, a dialectical relation that permits constructive criticism.

Show solidarity

If you believe in the objectives of the group or the community, demonstrate your belief through action. This is always the best form of communication. It is important to be able to defend the group's objectives convincingly, especially in a situation of conflict, when you may have to put yourself on the firing line. Taking a firm position in a meeting, signing a petition, or participating in a group's demonstration are all ways of showing solidarity. These gestures will not gain you immediate acceptance in a community different from your own, but they can build the trust that is essential for community work.

Know when you are no longer needed — or how to leave the community

While it is important to know how to become part of a community, it is equally important to know how to leave it when your work is done. Organizers must always keep in mind that they will have to leave the community one day, sometimes after many years. Unless they have hearts of stone, they will have developed friendships. But when the time is ripe, organizers must be prepared to direct their energies elsewhere lest they prevent the community from taking charge of its own affairs. This does not mean cutting all ties with the community; some form of contact can be maintained. The departure of the organizer from the community is like the end of a caseworker's involvement with a client, and it must be carefully prepared. Recall the final moments of the film "Norma Rae," when Joe, the union organizer who came from New York to organize a union in a plant in the southern United States, and who must leave to go elsewhere because duty calls, says goodbye to the heroine, played by Sally Field. That scene illustrates better than any words the importance, and also the difficulty, of leaving a community.

Conclusion: Why Do Community Work?

We will conclude this chapter by returning to the question of why studying the neighbourhood community is so important, particularly when many analysts, in Québec and elsewhere, have questioned the view of neighbourhood as centre of community life. In the age of the global village, citizens' groups are still promoting the small community. Some may see this as ridiculous or even dangerous, because in the final analysis it reinforces isolationism. In this view, to try to create community life in the neighbourhood is to attempt to artificially maintain a reality. In fact, community organizers in urban neighbourhoods far too often cling to a nostalgic vision of a vanished society in which the community still had meaning, basing their actions on the memory of a solidarity that supposedly existed in villages and neighbourhoods of old. But the desire to revive the feeling of belonging is difficult to maintain in the face of the harsh changes taking place, and many community organizers come to question the value of what they do.

The difficulties experienced by many organizers today on an individual and subjective level may be explained objectively by the profound social changes taking place. With the growth of urban mass society, social life in many communities has become impoverished. Organizers are being asked to revive urban community life and to infuse a "soul" into newly created neighbourhoods. In these circumstances, community work is discouraging and exhausting. Public authorities frequently give organizers or volunteers a mandate to "organize the community" or to "promote sociality." But increasing numbers of practitioners are wondering what is the point of trying to mend the social fabric when such powerful forces are working to tear it apart.[16]

In addition, since the beginning of the Eighties, the State has been trying to counter the rising costs of institutional services by a rediscovery of the value of volunteerism. In many areas of social policy, it is calling on the community to take responsibility for problems. All this, it seems to us, makes it necessary for organizers to clearly articulate their perception of the community with which they are working, and to make clear their conditions for partnership with the State. But it is not easy to develop new community organization practices, or even to sustain the established practices, when there is no official recognition or adequate funding of the work being done.

This situation has led to a reconsideration of both the objectives of community work and its political and ideological dimensions. With the changes that have taken place in local neighbourhoods, communities can no longer be seen as having clear physical boundaries. Community politics now takes place at a different level. People come together less out of a sense of belonging to a geographical area than out of a common desire to fight against various forms of domination or exploitation, or exclusion of specific groups, such as women, the elderly, or the handicapped. These new communities have the potential for uniting in broad coalitions to bring about social change.The old solidarity has not disappeared. In spite of social and economic change, most people still belong to networks of family, friends, neighbours, and co-workers that can be the source of both mutual aid and efforts at social change.

It seems to us that there is much to be gained from a renewal of the tradition of field studies from which community organizing originated. Even if the perfect model has yet to be found, we know that it must be situated somewhere between the overly strictly empiricism

of the monograph and the overly vague generalizations of pure interpretation. It is not an easy thing to understand a community well. A
very beautiful passage by Bertolt Brecht summarizes the philosophy
that should guide us.

> *So ends*
> *The story of a journey*
> *You have seen and you have heard*
> *You have seen what is common, what continually occurs*
> *But we ask you:*
> *Even if it's not very strange, find it estranging*
> *Even if it is usual, find it hard to explain*
> *What here is common should astonish you*
> *What here's the rule, recognize as an abuse*
> *And where you have recognized an abuse itself*
> *Provide a remedy!* [17]

NOTES

1. Martin Poulin, "L'etude monographique des communautes" in *Service social*, Vol. 27, No. 1 (Jan.- June 1978), pp. 85-100; C. de Robertis and H. Pascal, "L'étude de milieu" in *L'Intervention collective en travail social* (Paris: Le Centurion, 1987), pp. 112-35.

2. Jean Médard,*Communauté locale et organisation communautaire aux Etats-Unis* (Paris: A. Colin, 1969), p. 27.

3. *Studying Your Community*, 3rd ed. (New York: Free Press, 1969), cited in *ibid.*, p. 27.

4. Quoted in J. Duchastel, Marcel Rioux: "Entre l'utopie et la raison" (Montréal: *Nouvelle optique*, 1981)

5. Robert Couillard and Robert Mayer, "La pratique d'organisation communautaire à la maison de quartier de Pointe St-Charles" in *Revue internationale d'action communautaire*, No. 4/44 (1980), p. 114.

6. *L'Intervenant professionnel face à l'aide naturelle* (Chicoutimi, Qué.: G. Morin Editeur, 1984), p. 89.

7. "L'animation sociale en milieu urbain: une solution" in *Recherches sociographiques*, Vol. 6, No. 3 (1965), pp. 283-304.

8. Frédéric Lesemann, "Stratégies d'intervention auprès des individus et des collectivités: l'action communautaire" in *Les Cahiers de santé communautaire*, No. 2 (1979), p. 27.

9. "Comment ça marche, l'analyse sociale?" in *Relations* (Dec. 1982), p. 321. (Translators' note: This is a free translation.)

10. F. Sellier, "Le rôle des organisations et des institutions dans le développement des besoins sociaux" in *Sociologie du travail*, Vol. 12, No. 1 (Jan.-Mar. 1970), pp. 1-14.

11. B. de Cock and J. Grané, "Travail social et classes sociales" in J.P. Liégois, ed.,*Idéologie et Pratique du travail social de prévention* (Toulouse: Privat, 1977), pp. 137-98.

12. J. McKnight, (1977: 18).

13. Lesemann, *op. cit.*, p. 27.

14. Michel O'Neil, "Santé communautaire et communauté: de l'influence de deux conceptions de la communauté sur les interventions québécoises en éducation sanitaire" in *Les Cahiers de santé communautaire*, No. 2 (1979), p. 15.

15. M. Malavoy and N. St-Martin, "La formation pratique, ou apprendre dans l'action" in *Les Cahiers de recherche en travail social*, No. 23 (1982), pp. 111-22.

16. N. Baccouche, "L'intervention de l'intellectuel dans le social" in *Revue canadienne d'éducation en service social*, Vol. 5, No. 1 (1979), p. 8.

17. "The Exception and the Rule," Scene 8, in *The Jewish Wife and Other Short Plays*, trans. Eric Bentley (New York: Grove Press, 1965), p. 143. Quoted in Bernard Kayser, "Sans enquête, pas de droit de parole" in *Hérodote*, No. 9 (1978), p. 17.

COMMUNITY ORGANIZING:
Mobilization And Struggle

Community organizing starts with research, but its goal is action, usually in the form of a specific struggle. In Part Three, we will examine what is involved in organizing a struggle.

Before going to the heart of the subject, however, we warn against a potential pitfall for organizers: adventurism — the tendency to make action almost an end in itself, action for action's sake. We view adventurism as a sign of a potentially harmful political immaturity. Québec's recent history illustrates the dangers of certain types of actions carried out in the absence of popular support. Community organization aims precisely to allow communities and representative groups to decide for themselves whether to fight against oppression. It demands the utmost respect for the people with whom you work. Community organization is an educational process in which attitudes are just as important, if not more important, than skills. It should be a process of liberation, not only in its ends but also in its means. Things may take longer this way, but the results are more lasting.

This brings us to another consideration: the need for people to know what they are "getting into." An understanding of what is at stake and a determination to win, along with solidarity, are the essential ingredients for success in a struggle. To put it negatively, people must not feel that the wool is being pulled over their eyes or that they are being lied to. You must never lay yourself open to charges of manipulation, and if ever such charges are made, the people with whom you are working should be the first to deny them.

Our collective memory is not very good when it comes to recognizing what the popular movement has accomplished for our people since the beginning of the Sixties. Every group has a responsibility to contribute to the success of others' struggles by sharing its experience. It is also worth remembering that victories are to be celebrated and wounds nursed. Community organizing is carried out with and for human beings, usually the most oppressed. For them, a defeat can be crushing, and can lead to defeatism and demobilization. Yet, just as there is no total victory, there is no absolute defeat. Skill in nursing the wounds of members can be a decisive factor in ensuring that a group's activities continue. As for victories, celebrating is fine, but remember that boasting and swaggering are signs of weakness, not strength. Finally, it can be particularly painful when an organizer leaves at the end of a struggle, and we will deal with this delicate issue at the end of Part Three.

Community action is one stage in the complex process of community organization. Like research, it involves certain rules. Those discussed here represent the accumulated wisdom of the authors' practice over the last twenty years, as well as lessons that have come to us from the experience of our comrades elsewhere.

Five

MOBILIZATION:
Organizing a Group

Mobilization

Mobilization starts from a specific problem. It can be carried out on the basis of an existing group, or it may require that a new group be formed. There are two types of groups: those connected with institutions, and those that are independent. There are also two categories of unorganized people: those who are ready for action, and those who have not yet felt the need to act. Organizers should choose a mobilizing strategy on the basis of their research into the groups that exist in the community. They should also check to see if existing groups have the capacity to serve as a base for mobilization.

Mobilization on an institutional basis

The mobilization effort that led to the creation of the Coopérative d'action communautaire des citoyens de Hochelaga-Maisonneuve was carried out on an institutional basis. In this instance, the people in the community of Hochelaga-Maisonneuve were all using the Service d'économie familiale (Family Budget Service). The main form of their oppression, as identified by some organizers, was that the institutions were keeping them in a state of dependence. This dependence was related to the living conditions of the service's "clientele," who were mostly welfare recipients. After identifying the reasons that forced people to turn to the Family Budget Service for emergency aid, the organizers proposed that they form a group in which they would no longer be "clients," but take an active role as people working collectively to improve their living conditions.

The users of the service were called to a general meeting at which a plan for a cooperative was presented. A broader discussion developed, which allowed the organizers to test their hypotheses and to refine their plan in accordance with the people's comments. The people decided to bring action to bear on three levels. First, in terms of structure, they elected to set up a cooperative that would mainly include citizens representative of the community: welfare recipients, the unemployed, workers, housewives. In this way, they guaranteed themselves real control over their organization. Next, they decided on two specific types of activity. The first was to work collectively to improve their living conditions by establishing savings and educational programmes in areas they saw as particularly important, such as holidays, nutrition, and clothing. The second type of activity involved expressing solidarity with workers' and grass-roots struggles; this indicated a will to go beyond traditional local concerns.

The Citizens' Community Action Cooperative is a good example of successful mobilization. The objectives established by the organizers were met. Both autonomy and survival of the group were assured: the cooperative has now existed for thirteen years. This is an example of mobilization starting from an existing institution and on the basis of research done with the support of that institution. In this case the organizers belonged to the local community, sharing its aspirations and submitting willingly to the democratic decisions of the people. It should also be noted that the initiators of the project could not, with one exception, be considered professional organizers. However, as the project developed, some professional organizers were invited to collaborate, and they did so, generally conducting themselves very appropriately.

Mobilization on the basis of an independent group

Many organizers are connected with independent groups; they are both activists and staff of popular organizations. These groups are generally concerned with a relatively limited area of oppression. This is the case with ADDS (Association pour la défense des droits sociaux — Association for the Defense of Social Rights) groups, tenants' associations, and unemployed groups. Since in these cases organizers use the existing group as the basis for mobilization, the initial organizing phase will normally be relatively easy to carry out and the people mobilized will eventually be integrated into the group.

As an illustration, let us look at the appeal launched by ADDS to welfare recipients under the age of thirty. ADDS identified a problem specific to a particular segment of the population: extremely low benefits determined according to age. Not only do these people not receive enough money on which to live, but a basic principle of democracy is being violated, since if they do work, they are expected to pay the same income taxes as everyone else. In calling on these "young people" to mobilize, ADDS had two objectives: first, to make people aware of a very difficult situation and expose the hypocrisy of the State; and second, to make contact with a segment of welfare recipients that is often difficult to reach. ADDS read the situation accurately. This discrimination on the basis of age is arbitrary, and even contrary to the values enshrined in Québec's Charter of Rights and Liberties. Furthermore, in the current economic situation it is reasonable to expect that the possibilities for mobilizing young welfare recipients will be better than they have ever been.

While mobilization on the basis of an existing group enables that group to renew its membership and improve its power position in relation to the State and funding organizations, it may also reveal the need to set up a new, independent group. In the latter case, organizers must keep in mind that the long-term interests of the popular movement take precedence over the short-term interests of the groups that comprise it. Such situations have often occurred in the history of the popular movement. The development of a group into a Québec-wide organization has sometimes been stymied by localism or lack of vision or political judgement. It can also happen that organizers, fearing the development of a new leadership, try to control the new mobilization, or they may fear for their "job security." An organization of activists does not necessarily favour the same kind of structures as one of paid organizers. The purpose of these observations is to emphasize that mobilization on the basis of an established group can have effects not only outside the group, but also within the group itself.

Mobilization of people ready for action but not yet organized

Community organizers really show what they are capable of when they are working with the unorganized.

Sometimes the State or institutions provoke public outrage because of their obvious lack of concern for people or their outright dishonesty. The expropriation of farmland for the construction of Mirabel Airport, Hydro-Québec's admission that it intended to dam the Jacques-Cartier River, and Hydro's decision to build nuclear generating plants in Québec were all followed by this kind of reaction. Each of these actions by the State or one of its agencies created the potential for mass mobilization. The case of the Cercle d'économie de la future ménagère (Future Brides' Hope Chest) generated much interest a few years ago.

There is a role for the organizer when people are up against a company, and against the State as an ally of business. Mobilization is most effective when the people involved know they are "being organized." The issues in the conflict may not necessarily be clear, but the feeling of oppression is strong. It is as if the people are just waiting for a chance to express their anger and disapproval. This is where the organizer comes in.

Mobilization may begin with a public event organized by a State or private institution. In the case of the Future Brides' Hope Chest, for example, it began with the creditors' meeting. The organizer should not only know the case as well as possible, but should demonstrate to the participants in the meeting that it is in their interest to organize independently. This process will not be without risk since the people will have to face the opposition of those who have an interest in keeping them as disorganized as possible.

Mobilization of people who are not yet organized demands the utmost respect for democratic principles. The people must know that the organizer is not only competent but also committed to defending their interests. If they feel you are trying to get them involved in a rash experiment or manipulate them for ulterior motives, they will, with good reason, refuse to listen to your arguments or support your proposals. It is also a good idea to have your proposals legitimated by the meeting. It is not enough to say to people, "Anyone interested can leave their name and telephone number with so-and-so..." You should make certain before the hall is empty that at least some people have agreed to meet again soon on a specific date.

Further examples could be given of opportunities for mobilizing people who are conscious of being oppressed or exploited, such as the urea-formaldehyde foam insulation victims or the farmers expropriated at Mirabel. Organizers should be familiar with the history of the groups formed in these situations.

Mobilizing people who are not aware of their oppression

People are not born with political awareness. It is an understanding they acquire by thinking about and analyzing the causes of a situation being imposed on them contrary to their legitimate interests. It may happen that an organizer, after doing research, sees a need to mobilize a group of people or a particular segment of the population to fight a specific and obvious form of oppression. An example of this is the development in Little Burgundy of ADDS, a group that would later play a decisive role in the development of a Quebec-wide organization of welfare recipients.

The research of an organizer working for POPIR (Projet d'organisation populaire, d'information et de regroupement), in the southwest area of Montréal, showed that the community known as Little Burgundy was largely made up of welfare recipients. He noted that there was no organization to defend the rights of these citizens, and that community workers generally paid little attention to people on welfare. With the permission of his employer, he opened an office in the community and began checking out what resources he could count on in organizing welfare recipients. A community centre provided him with space, and a few activists from the Maison des chômeurs de St-Henri (St-Henri Unemployed House) agreed to work with him on a voluntary basis.

The chosen method of mobilization was to set up a special course. At this stage, the organizers did not know how many people would be interested in the initiative. As the project demonstrates, however, intuition and imagination can be important in organizing. The outline of the course was established and a funding proposal was presented to the Montréal Catholic School Commission under the title "Citizens and the Workings of Power." (This course was intended to be concrete, quite different from another course that was well-known during the same period, the late Sixties, entitled "Citizens and Power.")

The general idea was to start from people's awareness of their reality and, by explaining the workings of power, help them understand that this is not a matter of chance. The process involved the explanation of certain laws that to a great extent determined their living conditions. There was, for example, "Bill 26," which was nothing more nor less than a "collective agreement" imposed by decree on welfare recipients. Other laws governing housing, credit, health, and so forth were also analyzed with the assistance of resource persons whose credentials were undeniable since they were often government employees.

Other provisions were made, taking into account the characteristics of the target population. For example, it was decided that participants would be paid a nominal fee. The number of sessions was set at ten and the maximum number of "students" at twenty. A few people from neighbouring communities were accepted into the group. The organizers took the course along with the people who signed up. They acted essentially as catalysts for the rest of the group, a role that turned out to be decisive.

It became apparent, much to the surprise of the participants, that the law contained many provisions that were not generally known and that were not being applied. Government employees had been instructed by the ministry not to be too strict in the application of certain clauses involving allocation of money. This revelation served to raise the consciousness of the participants by several notches. Interestingly, the government employees who had been invited as resource persons discovered through this exchange with welfare recipients that they were being used as instruments of repression. A collaboration developed that eventually resulted in such accomplishments as the drafting of *Bill 26 Made Easy* by the welfare recipients.

Another important aspect of this mobilization was that the participants learned to value their own knowledge. They were not automatically assumed to be ignorant; rather, the emphasis was placed on what they knew. At the end of the course, a representative of a welfare group in Pointe St-Charles was invited to come and talk about her group's experiences. As a result of this process, part of the group decided to set up an information service for welfare recipients and to train themselves to become what would later be called "citizen welfare advocates."

It is beyond the scope of this book to analyze the many achievements of this project, but one essential fact should be emphasized: while it is possible to mobilize people who are oppressed without being conscious of it, it is essential that the mobilizing strategy take this factor into account. In other words, mobilization will succeed only to the extent that it is accompanied by consciousness-raising. The actions of groups fighting the oppression of women in its various manifestations are also revealing with regard to the need for consciousness-raising prior to mobilization.

As we have seen, there are many possible starting points for mobilization. But the choice of the basis for mobilization cannot be left to chance. It depends on the relationship the organizer has established with the community, the knowledge acquired through research, and the organizer's intuition and sensitivity to the community. In mobilization, you should avoid improvising — but if you must improvise, do it, as an actor does, after having mastered every line of the script.

We will now look at what happens once people have made the decision to get involved in a struggle.

Organizing a Group

Organizing a group is not easy. If mobilization has been success-ful, however, the solidarity that has already developed should make this stage less arduous. Here, again, the organizer plays a key role, particularly at meetings. The importance of the educational element in the actual organizational phase of community organizing cannot be overemphasized. Whether the group rapidly becomes independent or remains tied to the apron strings of its initiator depends largely on the political judgement of the organizer. When setting out to organize new groups, organizers should be very conscious of the fact that sooner or later, and usually sooner, they will have to leave. The implications of this will be discussed below.

Frequency of meetings

One of the first decisions to be made concerns the frequency of meetings. This may seem like a trivial point for someone who has nothing to do but attend meetings, but it can be a decisive factor in the vitality of a group. A few examples will illustrate this point. Your group will probably be made up of both women and men. Many of the women will be saddled with the double workload of job and housework; others will be full-time housewives with young children at home. As for the men, many will be working, sometimes at shift work. In addition, Saturday and Sunday are taboo, Friday is the night for shopping, there's hockey on Thursday, the most popular TV show is on Tuesday night at 8 o'clock, Monday is for laundry, and so on. And we have not even mentioned other activities in which members of your group might be involved, such as unions, bowling leagues, or school committees. All this to say that the frequency of your meetings is no minor issue. If you don't take these factors into account, people might just stay home. There is only one realistic way to solve this problem: check the availability of most participants, and then agree on a regular day.

You will then have to decide whether to meet once a month, bimonthly, or weekly. These decisions, while not carved in stone, have the advantage of enabling the members to make a place in their schedules for this new obligation. Any group starting out should do its utmost to avoid establishing a schedule of meetings that is too heavy for the majority of members. The group should be allowed to develop its ability to make decisions, and if the frequency of meetings needs to be changed, it is up to the members to change it.

Defining the organizer's role

This is particularly important in the case of a paid organizer working for an institution such as a CLSC (Local Community Service Centre). Will you be a full-fledged member? A resource person? An occasional guest? Your status in the group should be clearly defined from the beginning. Normally it will be whatever you want it to be. It is therefore important that you know the limits of your involvement. Whatever your choice, it should be based on such considerations as the interests of the group, your personal situation (married, children, other responsibilities), and the requirements of your employer.

It is best for you to explain to the group the reasons for your decision. This in itself can be educational, and can help the group advance in other areas such as the struggle against women's double workload. If you decide to ask to participate as a full-fledged member, your reasons may encourage less active members to become more involved. Here again, what is important is that you make those reasons clear.

Electing representatives

Those individuals assigned the task of representing the group are obviously key members. They should be chosen on the basis of their abilities, availability, and how representative they are of the group. Making this choice as democratically as possible does not preclude the possibility of particularly talented members being approached ahead of time and encouraged to run. Democracy is based on the principle that any member can run for office, without regard for such factors as their financial situation, gender, or physical attributes. Democracy does, however, allow encouraging certain people to run.

An important criterion is how representative a spokesperson is (representative in the political sense, and not in the sense that a lawyer represents a group in court or before a commission of inquiry). Imagine a sociology professor from the University of Montréal representing an organization of welfare recipients, or a student acting as spokesperson for a workers' organization — it would be strange, to say the least. The individual abilities of members should also be taken into consideration when representatives are chosen. Are they able to express themselves in public? Can they master the issues? Do they agree with the positions of the group? Are they energetic, determined, persuasive? Do the members identify with them? Take the case of a very militant women's group in the anti-pornography movement that chose as a spokesperson a woman who was prepared to accept so-called soft-core pornography. This actual example shows the importance of spokespersons having representative attitudes and abilities. Finally, one or several of your representatives must be available when needed.

We also caution against certain reprehensible practices. One example is "arm-twisting," getting people to run by playing on their emotions or telling them the mandate is only a formality. This practice is highly manipulative since it does not respect the person's freedom of choice. It also shows a weakness in the group — if you are reduced to arm-twisting to get people to represent you, it may be time to start worrying about the group's viability. Another unacceptable tactic is packing meetings. This practice is blatantly anti-democratic and shows serious problems in the organization of the group and in the ethics of the organizers. Any group that stoops to such practices discredits itself and does not belong in the popular movement.

A group's representatives give it its public image. A careless choice can cause irreparable damage to the group's credibility. It is also well worth the time and trouble to provide proper training for representatives.

Setting up committees

Committees are not only an indispensable instrument for carrying on the activities of a group, they are also an expression of the members' concern for democracy. There is no better way to involve a maximum number of people in an organization, especially since many committees do not require any particular skills. Committees that are more technical in nature can be assisted by resource persons.

Some committees should be formed as soon as possible, such as education, information, strategy, and finance committees. They are needed not only for organizational reasons, but also to get people to work. Through the work of the committees, the group's strategies and activities are developed, members demonstrate their talents, and leaders emerge. In addition — and this is particularly important — committees are excellent training grounds. That is why the resource persons who work with these committees should be chosen with care, taking into consideration such factors as their abilities, their understanding of the popular and union movements, their skills in popular education, their availability to contribute at certain strategic moments in a struggle — for example, to testify before a parliamentary commission or to speak as experts in other situations. The work of the committees should be treated seriously by all members. The popular movement, unlike the State, can't afford to waste time and energy.

Learning from the experience of others

More experienced organizers, the "old-timers" of community organizing, sometimes remark that younger organizers are starting from scratch, as if nothing had been done before they came along. There is a lot of truth in what they are saying, which is why, in the second part of this book, we emphasize the need to study the history of communities. The history of the popular movement, at least in its "modern" phase, now covers more than twenty years, and various types of organizing and kinds of action have already been tested. Much can be learned from the achievements of the popular movement.

Learning from the experience of others also means taking into account the existence of brother and sister groups, whose goals are similar to those of your group, and exploring the possibilities of working with them. What can you say about a group that tries to set up an association of welfare recipients without learning about the experience of ADDS, or someone who tries to set up a tenants' association, a community radio station, or a women's group without taking advantage of the experience of the many that already exist? Only that they are wasting precious time breaking their own trail when a road has already been cleared for them. Part of the organizer's job is to know about the popular movement and share that knowledge with the members of the group.

The experience of others can also be found in books and periodicals, films and videos. Organizers such as Saul Alinsky have written useful books and articles on community organizing. In Québec, too, there are many useful publications. The histories of groups, communities, and cities contain a vast store of valuable experience. Why not take advantage of them?

Work for everyone

Organizing a group means putting people to work, and that means there should be something for everyone to do.

Recently at a regional meeting of the Regroupement des Centres de Femmes (Federation of Women's Centres) a paid organizer asked the following question: "Why do all of you come to the regional meetings?" It was in the course of an evaluation of the relevance of the regional organization. One of the women responded, "There are forty of us in my group and nobody is interested in coming here, so I come." The organizer replied: "In that case, if your members are no longer interested in working on a regional basis, perhaps it would be better to stay there, and not come here if you don't know what you're coming here to do."

The organizer's reply may seem a little brusque, but she had a point. It is better not to have a group if the members don't know what they are doing in it. However, this is almost always the case for the first few meetings of a new group. Most of the people who have decided to join are shy and withdrawn. For many of them it is their first meeting and they have no experience with this kind of activity. An organizer should be aware of this and act accordingly. One way to handle the problem is to make sure everyone feels useful. You should also avoid snowing them under with the weight of your knowledge, making them think it takes a Ph.D. in administration or social work to belong to a popular group. Otherwise, you may soon find yourself with very few members.

There are no menial tasks in a group; they are all important. Contrary to what some might like to think, something as simple as calling members to let them know about a meeting or to remind them of the time and place is crucial. How many groups have had the experience of anxiously awaiting the arrival of the person who will make the quorum? How many organizers have found themselves with an attendance of two or three people when they were expecting at least twenty-five?

The importance of sharing tasks among a maximum number of members cannot be overemphasized. We warn against the tendency for organizers to accept all the "intellectual" jobs, or the tasks that the others think they are incapable of performing. Excuses such as "I don't have enough education to..." or "You do it, that's what you're paid for!" should be answered tactfully and firmly. Otherwise, you may be stuck with the role of "resident intellectual" for a long time. Obviously, for any number of reasons — education, understanding of the workings of power, experience working with groups — you are likely to be better equipped to perform certain tasks. The problem occurs not when you accept them for a certain period of time, but when you do them alone. It is essential that you pass on your knowledge. Members must work with you on tasks that they consider themselves incapable of doing. Tell them, "Alright, I'll do it, but somebody has to do it with me."

Determining what is possible

To put it simply, "Don't put the cart before the horse." There are two essential points to keep in mind: don't let yourself get dragged into activities that you won't be able to carry through for lack of sufficient membership, and always keep in mind the capacities of the members. The main concerns of a group that is just starting out should be consolidating the group and establishing a suitable structure. The activities of the group should be aimed at reinforcing its cohesiveness and clearly defining its objectives. To consider launching a major action when the group has only ten members, when no one has heard of it, and when nothing is really clear yet to the members themselves is to court disaster.

As soon as possible, the members should obtain all the information they will need to make choices and take informed decisions. Your members are not M.P.s or city councillors voting on subjects they know nothing about, and the popular movement should have nothing to do with such a caricature of democracy. For example, if you are mobilizing around housing and the group is aiming to set up a tenants' association, it would be appropriate for you as the organizer to tell them what your research has revealed about the landlord or landlords directly targeted by the group. It would also be relevant to outline the housing situation in the community, the situation with regard to land speculation, the existence of other tenants' associations and other possible allies, and the role of the Régie du logement (Québec Rental Board). Information can be presented in a lively and interesting way, and knowing about the achievements of other groups can be a stimulus to the members of your group.

All this is within the realm of possibility. On the other hand, an organizer who tries to get people involved in setting up a housing coop at the first or second meeting is dangerously out of touch with reality. Things must be taken one step at a time and placed in the context of a strategy that includes short-, medium-, and long-term objectives. There is no point in trying to skip stages.

Determining what is possible means taking into account the abilities of the members. This subject has already been discussed, so we will not go into detail. Remember, however, that while all the members are "learned" in their own ways, they also have their limitations. This is equally true of the organizer. It makes sense to take this into consideration when planning the programme of activities. As a general rule, every single activity should increase the members' ability to affect their environment. In other words, after each activity, the group should feel richer in understanding and solidarity. We know from experience that this is not always easy, but we feel that this concern should be one of the basic organizing principles for all groups in the popular and union movements.

The "tool" kit

The tools of popular groups are the material means they need to carry out their work — office, furniture, literature, telephone.

Some groups are desperately poor while others have more money. We know of no popular group that could be considered well off. On the other hand, many State institutions are very well funded. We will come back to this point; for now, suffice it to say that the usual situation for groups is poverty.

That should not prevent us from operating, however. Many groups are able to function very well with limited means. A group that is just starting to get organized can meet in a community centre, in a church basement, or in the offices of another group or a union. Members can use their home telephones. You should be wary of the temptation to wait until the group is well-equipped before becoming active. You should be all the more wary when there is no lack of government "job creation" projects around to discourage people from doing anything unless they are paid for it. People should come together on the basis of their common interest and will to take action. Only then, and only if it will improve the operation of the group, should they solicit funding for an office, staff, and other expenses.

When renting an office for a group, several factors should be taken into consideration. It should be centrally located for the convenience of the members, near a subway station or bus stop, and accessible to the disabled. Your furniture will most likely be secondhand. You can get it from the Salvation Army, or buy or borrow it from another group or an institution such as a school board.

Having a well-located office can be a stimulus to the group, especially if it is a pleasant place to meet. On the other hand, nothing is worse for the morale of the troops than having to meet in a pigsty. The popular Sixties slogan "Crud is not revolutionary!" still holds true. How many times have we had to hold meetings in rooms that were absolutely foul! It takes a petty-bourgeois mind to think that living in squalor is "getting close to the people." We hardly need to point out the contempt that such an attitude reveals. Equipment should also be well tended, keeping in mind that the group's tools belong to everyone. It is often advantageous for several groups to share services such as printing and copying.

The tool kit of a popular group is like that of a tradesperson: it's not so much the number of tools you have that is important, but how useful they are and whether you know how to use them. Most important of all, it's the skill of the worker that really makes the difference. You might have a spiffy office and all kinds of sophisticated gadgets, but they will not be of any use if your members don't know where they're going, if there's little solidarity, or if you don't have clear objectives.

Alliances

Groups should try to develop close relations with others pursuing the same objectives and also establish links with groups struggling on other fronts. Organizers who have done their research well know who their friends are. Alliances between groups not only build solidarity; they also make possible all sorts of exchanges, such as the sharing of various services.

Until the Seventies, citizens' groups tended to take a localist approach to issues. The welfare recipients of Pointe St-Charles had no contact with those in the south-central area of Montréal; organizers working in Montréal did not show much concern for their colleagues in Québec City; rural groups had few dealings with those in the city. Has the situation really changed? We would say "Yes, but..." Groups of welfare recipients, in spite of conflicts and tensions, have learned to talk to each other and to channel their energies into common struggles. It is not always easy, but it is being done. The same can be said for tenants' associations, consumer groups, food coops, and women's groups. There are still a few groups that resist the lure of solidarity, but in general there have been real changes in how popular groups relate to one another.

There are few indications that the same is happening with regard to relations between urban and rural groups. Organizations such as Au Bas de l'Échelle (Rank and File)[1] have on occasion taken part in training sessions organized by groups outside Montréal, but no close links have developed between city and country. There is definitely room for improvement.

The issue of alliances should come up as part of the process of organizing a new popular group. It is simply a matter of saving time and energy by taking advantage of the experience of others, and there is nothing dishonourable in an organizer suggesting that another group be consulted.

Using Institutions

CLSCs (Centres locaux de services communautaires —Local Community Service Centres), Social Service Centres, Adult Education Services, job creation programmes, the Office de protection du consommateur (Consumer Protection Bureau), the Conseil du statut de la femme (Québec Council on the Status of Women), and the Office des personnes handicapées (Disabled Persons Bureau) can be of help to popular groups. We would add to this list churches and church-funded organizations, volunteer bureaus, Centraide (United Way), and regional economic development organizations. A special place should be reserved for union federations and the Canadian Association for Adult Education. These institutions can provide you with valuable services if you know how to approach them and are aware of their limitations. We will briefly examine a few of them, but first we would like to make the following points.

Remember that CLSCs and legal aid offices are partly a result of the work of citizens' and popular groups. Some organizers have not gotten over the cooptation of their achievements and are still mistrustful of these organizations. It is prudent to approach State institutions with some skepticism, but you should also be able to adapt to changing circumstances. If you are aware of the role of these institutions, you can take precautions to maintain your independence while occasionally working with them. You should also be careful not to "burn" employees who work with you. They often take risks in order to help you, even to the point of jeopardizing their jobs, and you must understand and respect their limits.

CLSCs

Local Community Service Centres are the "front line" institutions of the health and social service network. Their activities fall into three areas: health, individual and group social services, and community services. Community organizing is part of the third area. Usually employees of CLSCs in working-class neighbourhoods are quite wiling to work with community groups. This collaboration must, however, fit in with the CLSC's programmes and priorities. For example, a doctor or a community worker could offer their services to a group of injured workers as long as their employer agreed. Otherwise, they would have to do it on their own time, or at their own risk.

CLSCs can be very useful to groups, although their capacity to take action in the community is limited by their very nature. They can offer anything from the loan of a vehicle to hiring a paid staff person to work in a certain area. They can help with research, provide resource persons for educational programmes or information sessions, and offer free meeting space or printing services. As long as the arrangements are clearly defined, CLSCs can provide useful back-up services for popular organizations.

Service d'éducation des adultes (Adult Education Service)

These institutions fill much the same role as CLSCs, but in education. There are Adult Education Services in school boards,

CEGEPs (junior colleges), and universities. They can help in developing educational programmes, provide access to funding, and supply resource persons for workshops and information meetings. In Montréal, they finance the Centres d'éducation populaire (Popular Education Centres), which provide many groups with low-cost office and meeting space. School boards are sometimes very bureaucratic, but the SEAs can still be a valuable resource.

Centres de services sociaux (Social Service Centres)

CSSs can provide only social workers. With the current cuts in the social services network, the number of community workers hired by these centres has been drastically reduced. They specialize in casework. Sometimes, however, you may find useful resources in the area of information and education.

Bureaux d'aide juridique (legal aid offices)

Some legal aid offices are quite willing to help popular groups. Consumer groups, for example, can often get technical help from them. Under Québec law, if you are a non-profit group, you are entitled to free services — for example, in incorporating your group. You can also ask for a legal aid mandate to hire the lawyer of your choice, if necessary.

Canadian Association for Adult Education

Unlike CLSCs, the CAAE cannot provide concrete services, but it can offer valuable support in its own field, such as backing the demands of community groups for adequate funding for popular education. In other areas, such as communications, the CAAE plays a role that few community organizations are capable of filling. It has done research on the effects of new technologies on social relations, in particular the oppression of entire populations through the manipulation of ideas by the mass media. This is not something organizers are usually concerned with on a daily basis, but media manipulation can have a considerable effect on you and the people with whom you work.

The CAAE's concern with these issues and the research it does are of great value.

Union federations

Many writers have emphasized the special relationship that should exist between the union movement and the popular movement. We are forced to admit, however, that this relationship is more a wish than a reality. It does not occur spontaneously. When setting up a new group, organizers should keep in mind the advantages of developing links with unions. First, it is very likely that some members of the group will be union members. Their involvement in both movements should help them understand the relation between the exploitation of their labour and their oppression in other situations. Another important reason for popular groups to join forces with the union movement is that the union movement is currently the only organized force with enough political clout to occasionally counter the power of the State. In the current context of wage concessions and non-indexation of unemployment and welfare benefits, anything the popular movement can do to strengthen the union movement can only be beneficial. Moreover, you should be aware that the State has an interest in turning popular social groups — youth, welfare recipients, the elderly, women — against unionized workers. This becomes abundantly clear during labour conflicts in the public sector. To be unaware of these tactics is to weaken both the unions and the popular movement.

Expressions of solidarity between union and popular movements are always welcome, and initiatives such as the Sommets populaires (Popular Summits), common fronts, exchanges of technical and educational resources, regional coalitions, and joint demonstrations should be encouraged. When organizing a group, you should always include active solidarity in the programme of activities.

Other resources

It is important to mention a few of the organizations that serve the interests of the union and popular movements. The Centre de formation populaire (Popular Training Centre), which has been in existence since 1972, provides educational resources and activities. The Centre populaire de documentation (Popular Resource Centre) is a gold mine of information on all kinds of subjects related to the labour and popular movements. Organizers will find resources and considerable technical expertise in these and similar organizations.

NOTES

1. Translators' note: Rank and File is a group that works to defend the rights and improve the working conditions of non-unionized workers.

Six

ORGANIZING A STRUGGLE

Popular groups and organizations have two main purposes, which in our view complement each other and which are basically the same as those of the trade union movement: service and struggle. In this book, we deal only with the latter, the role of popular groups in fighting for social change.

We are certainly not claiming that all groups identify with this definition; they often see themselves very differently. However, it seems clear that, leaving aside the reservations some groups might have about using words like "struggle," "fight," and "demand," the definition fits. For example, when a group that sees itself as primarily concerned with recreation and self-help pickets the Centraide (Québec equivalent of the United Way) offices to demonstrate against bureaucratic requirements of that funding organization, what is it doing? Take the case of a group that carefully avoids the word "struggle," but signs several petitions a year demanding the use of a vacant lot for housing rather than industry or business, calling for an empty school to be used for the community, opposing plans to demolish rental housing or cuts in health and social services or the freezing of salaries and benefits. What are they doing if not associating themselves with the struggles of other groups? Beyond the snares of words, there is the reality of oppression, and the will, not always expressed, to fight it. This is what we are talking about when we use the word "struggle."

In the following pages, however, we will discuss "struggle" in a narrower sense, as deliberate action carried out by a group against an identified form of oppression. Examples of this kind of action include the struggle of ADDS (Association for the Defense of Social Rights) against welfare recipients being forced to pay the Montréal water tax, the struggle of the expropriated farmers of Mirabel to recover their land, the urea-formaldehyde foam insulation victims' fight for compensation, the young welfare recipients' fight for decent benefits, the women's anti-pornography campaign, the struggle of the people of the Lower St. Lawrence to protect their environment, and the fight of native peoples for their rights. As even this very selective list shows, struggle is a reality for a great many people.

Setting Objectives

When the members of a group decide collectively to get involved in a struggle, they must go through a process of thinking, questioning, and consciousness-raising in order to better understand their particular oppression. They know that they are being subjected to an injustice, by whom and why, and their consciousness of that injustice makes it intolerable. They can no longer accept it, so they decide to fight it.

Initiating a struggle requires that you know your objectives. Normally, these involve bringing the situation of injustice to the public's attention and getting it corrected. The objective of the struggle by women (and a few men) against pornography, for example, is to put an end to the practice of reducing women to objects for consumption. This is not the only goal, however. There are also educational objectives, such as helping women understand their oppression and showing men the infantile nature of pornography, the violence it expresses, and the economic interests it serves. Another objective of the struggle might be to strengthen solidarity among women in general and organized women's groups in particular. Finally, this struggle has the potential to become a major political battle.

In general, objectives are either immediate or long-term. Immediate objectives are those you would like to see achieved at the end of a particular struggle. For example, in the case of pornography, an immediate objective might be to stop the hiring of nude female dancers by a particular club. The long-term objective would be the elimination of pornography in all its forms. To take another example, one related to urban planning, a popular group struggling on this front might first demand the demolition of a few firetraps in its neighbourhood, and aim in the long term for the adoption of a renovation policy for the whole city.

Let us look a little more closely at the question of objectives. It is always important, when initiating a struggle, to set some goals that are relatively easy to attain. In other words, our objectives must not be so broad that they are, in the end, unattainable. Nothing is worse for the morale of a group than not having any successes. A struggle is a process, and each stage has its own objectives. When the members meet to evaluate their strategy, they must be able to see precisely what gains have been made during each stage of the process. Obviously, they will be motivated to continue the struggle if they know they are making progress. Many struggles have had harmful effects on groups, usually because the objectives were poorly defined or overly ambitious.

The organizer should also know that while it is essential for members to have a clear idea of the goals being pursued, there is also a level of objectives that might be considered intrinsic to any struggle. These are the effects that can be expected in terms of strengthened solidarity within the group and with its allies, increased possibilities for recruiting new members, and improved funding. Not everyone may be aware of these objectives, but the organizer should take them into account.

Strategy and Tactics

A strategy is an organized effort to influence a person or an institution in order to achieve a specific objective. Tactics are the means used to attain the objectives, or, to put it another way, to carry out the strategy. The tactics should therefore be consistent with the strategy —

that is, they must be appropriate to the type of objectives being pursued, in both the short term and the long term.

How the requirement for consistency is applied will depend on the philosophy of the group. A group can be so "pure" that it risks failure or loses control of an action. Refusing to take money from a funding organization that does not share the group's goals or to use media controlled by the bourgeoisie are decisions that might be made in the context of a particular strategy. The opposite decision in these circumstances, however, may also be a tactical choice: one that respects the strategy while appearing temporarily to deviate from it, the better to succeed in the long-term struggle. We speak of a tactical alliance when a group allies itself with individuals or groups that do not share its long-term goals but only certain short-term objectives. For example, a tenants' association might be able to use the Rental Board against landlords, even if the Board itself is one of its targets for change. A group of women using a Social Service Centre could ally themselves with the centre to denounce cuts in services by the State. The art of tactics consists in being flexible without distorting your strategy or losing sight of your objectives.

The following factors should be taken into account in determining strategy: 1) the socio-political and economic situation; 2) the strengths and weaknesses of the popular movement and its allies; 3) the strengths and weaknesses of the opponents and their allies; 4) the goals of the popular movement; 5) the group's long-term goals and the steps required to achieve them. A strategic analysis of these factors will enable a group to develop a coherent set of tactics.

Once the analysis has been completed and the long-term goals defined, a group should decide what action it will take, not only to obtain better conditions for its members, but also to increase the power of the popular movement. The action should be directed against a concrete, immediate problem. It should relate to the everyday lives, at home or at work, of the people in the community being organized. The short-term objectives should be clearly defined. An example of such an action is the fight for traffic lights on Esplanade Street in Montréal. This was a dangerous street because of heavy traffic, but it was a residential street and often served as a playground for neighbourhood kids, since the area was distinctly lacking in recreational facilities. In addition, children used the street to go to and from school. In this situation, children's safety was an objective to which the residents were likely to rally. The concrete demands were traffic lights, street signs, and better control of traffic. There was a potential for other demands to emerge in the context of the struggle, such as the development of recreational facilities in the neighbourhood.

This example illustrates the point that an action should be part of a process that aims to satisfy both collective and individual interests. Mobilizing for a principle or a right that does not directly affect oneself is a luxury few can afford. Action should therefore respond to a need that is felt by the population. In our example, the collective interest required that the dangerously high volume of traffic be reduced. All the residents had a personal interest in the safety of their children and in their own peace of mind. Those without children would gain in quiet and tranquility.

Objectives must be within reach. There is no point in making great efforts if there is no chance of success. Remember that people are already busy with everyday responsibilities. The Regroupement pour le gel des loyers (Coalition for a Rent Freeze) had problems mobilizing people because its goal seemed distant and unattainable in the context of our society. In addition, the legitimacy of the goal was not easy to demonstrate, since most people probably consider it normal that rents should go up with inflation. The group finally had to resign itself to putting this demand on the back burner.

By way of contrast, the struggle of ADDS against welfare recipients being forced to pay municipal water tax was an undeniable success. In 1974, many groups and community organizers felt that this struggle was doomed to fail because of the scope of the demand, which was addressed to both the City of Montréal and the Québec ministry of social affairs. It also required that participants take serious risks: welfare recipients could have had part of their benefits seized, or their water cut off (as occurred in the municipality of Pointe-aux-Trembles). The issue had strong emotional appeal and symbolic value, however, because of the abhorrent nature of these repressive measures. It was only with strong support from other groups and organizations, and solid legal back-up, that the original core group of activists managed to build a broad mobilization and finally score a victory. This example shows that an objective can be difficult to attain and still be realistic. A whole series of factors must be evaluated when setting objectives.

An objective should have a moral aspect to appeal to the public and the media. It is easy to denounce cutoffs by Hydro-Québec, for example, since the public considers electricity an essential service. Sexual harassment of female welfare recipients by welfare officials also has a clear moral angle. Actions against fraudulent business practices, a boycott against a company that closes a factory, and protests against cuts in essential services are examples of actions that appeal to ethical principles.

Similarly, an objective must be "hot." A period of economic recovery is not as good a time to campaign against unemployment as a period of recession. A tax hike provides a good opportunity to denounce waste in government. The Taxe-action group in Montréal mobilized many small property-owners when they received their tax bills. A tax revolt had begun and many people sought an organization through which to channel their individual anger. Unfortunately, the initiators of the movement did not follow up on this revolt, and were not able to organize in significant numbers.

An objective should also contain an emotional element. The recent action of women welfare recipients against male welfare officials who were abusing their authority is an excellent example of a situation with an emotional appeal, one that generated anger and gave rise to a strong will to fight.

One last important criterion in the choice of objectives is educational content. Beyond the concrete results achieved, the long-term educational results should be considered. A struggle is an opportunity for learning, for gaining a better understanding of the workings of society in general or of a specific institution. Presenting a brief to a parliamentary commission in an attempt to influence legislation can be very instructive, even if the action has very little impact on the government. It offers an opportunity to better understand the political game, the importance of power relations, and the limits of a certain kind of democracy.

These criteria should not be applied rigidly, but rather serve as guidelines for developing a strategy for collective action. There must be a continual evaluation of the tactical requirements of a given strategic choice on the various actors involved. This evaluation demands sensitivity to everyone involved in the struggle.

Evaluate the solidity of the group's roots, and start with low-risk actions. It is also important to respect the "local culture." The women's movement, for example, had to be sensitive to women's fear of physical violence (a fear that, we might add, is by no means exclusive to women; but the women's movement at least had the intelligence to take it into account). The group's style must be respected so that people feel at ease and even enjoy participating. It's hard to imagine the welfare recipients in ADDS presenting a brief to a parliamentary commission with all its protocol. Negotiations in the office of a lawyer or a government minister tend to exclude and demobilize working-class members of a group.

Respect the size and strength of the group. You do not organize a demonstration with thirty people, but it is quite reasonable to organize a delegation of thirty to meet a representative of the opposing party.

Consider the momentum of the action. Recognize that there are strong periods and weak periods, and allow time for rebuilding strength. Following an important meeting, people need to catch their breath and take stock; they cannot keep up a breathless pace for very long. Finally, the same tactic should not be used and re-used ad nauseam.

Public support is essential: the group should maintain its good image, and expose its adversaries for what they are. In order to win public support, you must respect people's intelligence and appeal to their understanding. A public sector strike is never popular and can provoke a very negative reaction unless it is preceded by a long information campaign and unless the public feels that there are common interests between itself and the strikers. A demonstration blocking traffic or preventing access to a public place should be clearly explained as a last resort in support of a just demand. Public sympathy is absolutely necessary in struggles against the State. If you forget this principle, you risk doing a disservice to your own cause and to the popular and union movements.

The target: clearly identify the Achilles' heel of your adversary, and then choose the appropriate means of attack. The means chosen may be ridicululous for a person or a prestigious institution. You may choose to force your adversary to respect its own rules — an institution that prides itself on its democratic methods looks bad if it refuses to make information available. It always hurts to be reminded of one's principles when one fails to respect them. The threat of an action can often be more effective than the action itself, if the adversary believes that the group is capable of carrying out the threat. The apparent irrationality of a group of workers might frighten the boss, especially if their union says it cannot control its troops. It takes continual pressure to break resistance; therefore, while varying the action in order to keep things interesting, maintain the pressure.

Beyond these considerations, try to follow the established plan in terms of strategy and long-term objectives. It is important to check tactics against basic criteria to ensure that they are consistent with the strategy. The group should ask itself the following questions:

-Is the action important enough to carry the group forward to the next step to the long-term objectives?

-Are the issues clear?

-Are the threats credible?

-Will the action shake up the adversary or put it off guard?

-Will the action get our message across, both to the adversary and to the general public?

-Will the action be fun for the participants?

-Are there alternative actions in case the first choice does not work?

-Have we solicited all possible support?

-Have we ensured that we will meet the adversary on ground where we feel at ease, and according to a timetable we control?

-What are the legal constraints on the action? (It is important to foresee potential problems and arrange for appropriate resources.)

-*What are the potential effects of an action? Is there a risk that it might lead to an over-reaction?*
-*What material resources are required?*
-*Can the follow-up for the action be planned immediately?*
-*What effect will the action have on the organizational base of the group?*

Questions like these will help you avoid tilting at windmills. They should not, however, serve as an excuse for doing nothing. While it is sensible to ask questions, this can also become a way of avoiding responsibility. If you wait to have all the answers before you take action against oppression and exploitation, you may never lift a finger, since there will always be that one question you can't answer.

Tactics

Saul Alinsky laid down a series of rules, which he used as guidelines in planning his actions. In Alinsky's view of power relations, the Have-Nots are constantly trying to win more power, and their only resources are their numbers and almost no money. The two main sources of power, according to Alinsky, are money and people, and tactics means doing what you can with what you have. In keeping with Alinsky's scorn for all dogma, we should emphasize that his rules are not absolute; their application depends on context. It is important to be able to change your mind when you make a mistake, either with regard to the target or in judging the power required.

Here are are Saul Alinsky's rules of power tactics:

First rule: Power is not only what you have but what the enemy thinks you have.
Second rule: Never go outside the experience of your people.
Third rule: Wherever possible go outside the experience of the enemy.

Fourth rule: Make the enemy live up to their own book of rules.

Fifth rule: Ridicule is man's most potent weapon.

Sixth rule: A good tactic is one that your people enjoy.

Seventh rule: A tactic that drags on too long becomes a drag.

Eighth rule: Keep pressure on with different tactics and actions, and utilize all events of the period for your purpose.

Ninth rule: The threat is usually more terrifying than the thing itself.

Tenth rule: The major premise for tactics is the development of operations that will maintain a constant Pressure upon the opposition.

Eleventh rule: If you push a negative hard and deep enough it will break through into its counterside (for example, Gandhi's tactic of passive resistance).

Twelfth rule: The price of a successful attack is a constructive alternative.

Thirteenth rule: Pick the target, freeze it, personalize it, and polarize it.[1]

Alinsky also emphasizes that once you have reached the decision to engage in a battle, assume that the cause being defended is one hundred percent positive and the opposition is one hundred percent wrong.

There are countless possible tactics. It is essential that you use your imagination to constantly develop new means that are effective and, if possible, enjoyable. Tactics can be divided into the following categories: confrontations within established norms, violations of social norms, and violations of legal norms.

Confrontations that are acceptable according to social norms are forms of protest like public debates and legal battles. These means can be used following unsuccessful negotiations — in a labour dispute, for example. Opposition can also take the form of petitions, letters to the editor, demonstrations, picketing, and press conferences. It can also be advantageous to play on divisions in the opposing camp; political parties, in particular, are always happy to attack each other. Another form of pressure on the adversary is "overuse" of a service, or strict and overzealous respect for rules. Welfare recipients can all call their welfare officers the same day for an appointment. Employees can seriously inconvenience their employer by overzealousness.

Violations of social norms are more delicate and should be approached with caution. You won't achieve anything if you deliberately antagonize the public; here we are thinking of strikes, especially in the public sector. Methods that use non-cooperation usually aim to either attract public attention or prevent the opposing forces from operating normally. A national day of solidarity, with everyone staying home from work, is a particularly powerful way of dramatizing a cause. Boycotts, if they are well organized, can be very disruptive; examples include the boycott of California produce in support of the demands of farm workers there and, in Québec, boycotts of the postal code, of Cadbury products, and of Firestone tires. The success of such tactics depends essentially on the public's response.

Finally, tactics can violate legal norms. In this case, the consequences must be carefully weighed. The imprisonment of Québec union leaders a few years ago was the rather spectacular result of their use of such tactics. The aim is always to stop the adversary from functioning, and/or to make them look bad. The occupation of a public place or a factory is a violation of legal norms. The offices of government ministers are ideal for this kind of action. Refusing to pay taxes, refusing to circulate, or disrupting a trial are tactics that can lead to problems for those who adopt them, but they can also result in victory.

These examples give only an idea of the variety of tactics one can use. It is important that the tactic chosen be understood by those who decide to use it.

Negotiation

Negotiation is an example of the tactics involved in a strategy of confrontation in community action. Developed mainly in the area of labour relations, negotiation is also used by popular groups.

Popular groups often have to contend with representatives of government or funding agencies who do not share their views on a whole range of subjects, such as legislation, development plans, and funding procedures. They often negotiate for financial benefits or changes in legislation. The contexts and the forms of negotiation can vary widely. Saul Alinsky, who served his apprenticeship in the union movement, relates several experiences in labour negotiations from which he drew his tactical methods. We borrow from both his experience and that of the Québec union movement, which has established principles applicable to any negotiation, whatever the goal.

Negotiation can be either the starting point or the end result of collective action. We see it in the context of conflict in which the parties have different objectives but share a common will to reach an agreement. The definition of negotiation we have adopted is the following: a process that takes place between two parties for the purpose of reaching an agreement on a particular issue or subject of disagreement. It can either be a genuine attempt to present one's objectives to the opposing party or to the public, or simply a delaying tactic. For the purposes of this book, we are assuming serious negotiations intended to culminate in a real agreement. We should also specify that these negotiations can be explicit or implicit, i.e. carried out through statements and indirect communications, with each party sending up "trial balloons" that imply certain positions, but without any face-to-face confrontation.

In explicit negotiations between a popular organization and a public institution, a representative of the government, or a business that controls significant economic resources, two factors have to be taken into consideration: the respective resources of the parties and the formulation of demands.

In order for there to be real negotiations, both parties must have enough resources to give them a degree of power, and each party must be able to impose sanctions on the other. Popular groups usually have far fewer resources than the authorities with whom they are negotiating. Essentially, their power depends on their capacity to marshall public opinion and/or to disturb social peace and order. They may also possess information that the opposing party does not want made public. Finally, they can contrast the legitimacy of their demands with the arbitrary actions of the opposing party. The administrations of public and private institutions have definite advantages. They hold the purse strings, they have access to information on groups, and they can use force. In order to increase its bargaining power, a group can use a dramatic action. Such actions help mobilize the members of the group, attract public attention, and serve as an indication of the group's determination. They also represent an opportunity to bring the members of the group closer together before a period of long, hard negotiations.

It is not the purpose of this book to list all possible tactics, but we will mention a few that can be effective in exposing contradictions and that are consistent with democratic principles. For example, it can be very embarrassing for civil servants when a group goes directly to a government minister to denounce an interfering or incompetent bureaucracy. Likewise, the board of directors of a CLSC may find itself being reminded of the values that are supposed to govern the establishment it administers. Civil servants who pride themselves on their sensitivity to the concerns of ordinary people can be put on the spot if the facts reveal that they are enforcing repressive policies. How many landlords will settle rather than waste their time at the Rental Board? Petitions and letters to the editor are also means that can help speed up negotiations.

Finally, victory often goes to the party that is able to put up with the insults, the wear and tear, and all the little annoyances. That party must demonstrate a great deal of strength and cohesiveness, and always show that it is ready to go into action. This is where the internal communications of the group are important. There should be good channels of communication between the negotiators and the other members of the group, so that the group is continuously involved in the negotiation process. The negotiating team needs to feel the kind of total support that is only possible when there is a clear mandate.

The opposing party will try to divide the negotiators. It will say that some of them do not represent the group, or attempt to use certain kinds of arguments to appeal to those it thinks can be won over. Beware of the danger of having an organizer or advisor whose education or social origins are similar to those of the opposing party. The adversary will try to appeal to the "superior knowledge" and "sense of responsibility" of this negotiator, asking him or her to talk sense into these "poor people" who understand nothing about institutional constraints. It may be preferable for an advisor in this position to play a background role and leave the control to those negotiators who are more representative of the organization and its constituency.

The community organizer who has been given a mandate as an advisor should use this position of "independence" to maintain the distance necessary for analysis and for educating the members of the group on the game of negotiation. The group should carry out the negotiations itself, even if at times this is very difficult. Technical jargon can be a trap to divert you from the real issues. Keep your eyes fixed on the real objective of the group and do everything to attain it. You can think about the paperwork and the technicalities later.

The formulation of demands is an important aspect of the negotiation process. Often the final result depends more on the formulation than on the merit of the demands. The rule is that you begin by demanding one hundred and fifty percent of what you would agree to, and the other side begins by offering fifty percent. Why such a distortion? Making extreme demands helps compensate for the disadvantage of being the one asking for something. It forces the other party to reveal its position. You ask for a rent freeze, free universal daycare, or free education at all levels, and the opposing party, in this case the State, has to respond and explain the reasons for its counter-offer or its refusal. Negotiating from extreme positions lets you probe for openings. What is not said openly is often important in the give-and-take of negotiations, and demands, offers, and counter-offers are clues to the limits and the priorities of each party. The offers and demands define the limits. For example, the Common Front[2] asked for minimum weekly wages of $100, $165, and then $265 for the first year of the contract during their negotiations in 1972, 1976, and 1979. These demands were met by the end of each contract. They constituted major gains not only for public sector workers, but also for private sector workers and for the entire popular movement.

Be careful not to go overboard in formulating demands, nonetheless, or you won't be taken seriously. Overstatement is not always the best tactic. You must know how to be honest and credible in any kind of negotiations. You should also hold back some trump cards to use at the right moment. Similarly, certain low-priority demands may eventually be put aside in favour of more important ones. Pushing too hard on a minor issue can cause a general hardening of positions and destroy the possibility of concessions in other areas.

Finally, in the case of demands that are known to the public, the image of moral rightness is always important. The wage demands of the Common Front were supported by figures on the cost of living; they were so obviously just that they readily won public support.

One last point to consider is whether the group should suggest solutions to the problem it is protesting. Should the users of services be expected to do the work of the experts? This depends on various factors. It is certainly valuable to know what you want and to have possible solutions. Perhaps it is not relevant to share these "findings" with those you are fighting, but it may turn out to be necessary to answer to public opinion.

Negotiation consists of bluff and pressure. It can, however, take place in an atmosphere of diplomacy and tact. What is particularly important is to anticipate as much as possible the actions and reactions of the opposing party. It is therefore essential to accurately assess the objectives of the other side and to be able to evaluate their relative strength at any time. The balance of power can change over time, and it is important to seize the opportunity for an opening or for a threat. But you must be careful. A negotiator who is ready to concede a point may backtrack if too heavy a threat is made.

Threats must always be credible; that is, they must be in proportion to the importance of the issue and you must be capable of carrying them out. Unfortunately, we live in a world in which the carrot and the stick reign. Those in power have repeatedly shown their readiness to abandon their principles when it comes to taking care of their own interests. Québec provides many examples of the hypocrisy of politicians, such as the declaration of the War Measures Act in October 1970, the referendum on sovereignty, and elections. This is not the world in which we want to live, but we cannot afford to be naïve or holier-than-thou. Community organizing seeks change; we must not allow ourselves to be trampled because we do not dare answer our adversaries with the same weapons they unhesitatingly use against anyone who threatens their peaceful enjoyment of privilege and power.

This brings us to another important consideration, the writing up of the agreement. It is often said that everything should be in writing so that there is no room for doubt. However, the lack of an official written agreement can sometimes mean more substantial gains. Your memory (confirmed by unofficial notes) can clarify the interpretation of the agreement; this can sometimes make possible concessions that cannot be officially acknowledged. If there is no climate of trust, however, or in the absence of credible witnesses who can guarantee that the agreement will be respected, you should be firm about demanding a clear official text.

It is extremely important that the negotiators prepare for negotiating meetings — by role-playing, for example. A chief spokesperson should be designated and the role of each team member decided. In some cases, it is best to assign responsibilities according to the skills of the negotiators, with some presenting the issues and others providing details on various important aspects. Whatever the division of tasks, it is essential to present an image of consistency and cohesiveness. If there is any uncertainty, it is best to ask for a halt to the proceedings so you can clarify your position. You must maintain control of the pace of negotiations, and not permit constraints to be imposed that may handicap your position.

Negotiations often take place under circumstances that are disadvantageous to popular groups. It is important, before starting, to carefully choose the site of the negotiations and to decide on the time to allow for them. Never let yourself be intimidated by the atmosphere of a place or by formalities or other gimmicks intended to impress, and be wary of being trapped by the language of the adversary. It is easy to say nothing with a lot of beautiful words, and many politicians and technocrats are skilled at this game.

To sum up, before negotiating the following must be clearly defined: high-priority and low-priority demands, acceptable and unacceptable concessions, arguments in support of the demands, degree of firmness to be maintained, "trump cards" and "bargaining chips," and the strengths and weaknesses of each party.

Negotiation has not become established as a practice in community organizing. However, it is sure to be developed further as the working class is increasingly obliged to defend its interests against the State. Groups for the defence of rights and interests should be able to make their points of view heard in the forums where the major issues of the day are discussed and decisions taken that affect us all. If we do not want to be totally manipulated, we must develop the strength and the methods to influence decisions. Negotiation is one such method, but it can be effective only to the extent that we represent a significant organized force.

The art of retreat

A struggle is not a game: you want not only to play, you want to win. Popular groups should not push the sporting spirit so far as to go into a fight knowing full well they are going to lose, or that they are going to gain nothing.

When faced with imminent defeat, it is important not to go any further. It is wiser to make a tactical retreat to avoid being crushed by your adversaries. Retreat is not defeat. It is a tactic that lets you return to a more comfortable position from which you can adjust your strategy and continue the struggle. The best example of a situation for retreat is the arrival of a contingent of police during the occupation of a public building.

The place to which you retreat should be established ahead of time. It could be a rented hall where members and their friends retreat for a party; or a press conference could be held to denounce the attitude of an adversary who, instead of negotiating, calls the police. Such an event can even work to your advantage by providing an opportunity to draw public attention to your struggle.

When you must retreat, it is important to do so in an orderly way and, if possible, with good humour. Members must understand that this is not a defeat but simply a stage in their struggle.

Tasks

When we spoke of the organization of a group, we emphasized the need to share tasks among a maximum number of people. In the course of a struggle, the organizer should be all the more concerned with the division of tasks since this is an important factor in building solidarity, and success depends in large part on the quality of that solidarity. Here, once again, there are no unimportant tasks. Whether participating in a phone tree, leafletting, or representing the group at a press conference, everyone's role is important.

Two words sum up the importance of a good division of labour: cooperation and commitment. For a member, taking on a concrete task in the struggle is proof of commitment, a way of accepting a share of the responsibility, and an affirmation of the importance he or she places in the struggle. Distributing tasks can be an opportunity to use creative tactics. During the boycott of California grapes, it was common to see groups of nuns leafletting customers at the entrance to a supermarket. Needless to say, people were more interested in taking the leaflets than if they had been distributed by a bunch of teenagers. Similarly, an occupation of an elected official's office by senior citizens is more effective than one by students. Whatever task a member agrees to take on, it goes without saying that he or she should be well informed as to what is involved.

The natural abilities and acquired skills of individual members should be taken into account when assigning tasks. Everyone is not equally qualified to represent the group publicly. Similarly, certain members will be more skilled at handling the technical aspects of an issue when dealing with a well-prepared adversary. This does not mean that only "experts" should be given the roles of spokespersons or negotiators. Far from it. It does mean, however, that the skills of each member be identified and used wisely.

Finally, there is nothing more despicable than an organizer who hides behind others, who refuses to get involved in humble tasks, or who runs away at the slightest danger. And the organizer who wants to play the "big leader" has no place in a struggle.

Solidarity

It is solidarity that fuels popular groups. We do not mean merely formal solidarity, but rather the concrete expression of fellowship and sharing among equals. *Esprit de corps* is essential to a group involved in a struggle. It is demonstrated in small ways, or in what seem like small ways. For example, let us say a member of the group is in hospital. Have you provided for a way to keep him or her informed of what is going on? Have you thought of giving him or her certain tasks to do, such as making a few phone calls or addressing envelopes?

Empathy can also mean taking into account the fears of certain members or respecting their desire not to commit themselves, in whole or in part, to a struggle. Solidarity is not judgemental. A few years ago, we heard some women social workers belittling women members of popular groups who had refused to associate themselves with "their" March 8 activities. Rather than questioning the relevance of the kind of activities they had organized, rather than trying to understand the reasoning of the other women, the social workers preferred to spout slogans such as "Your kitchen walls are blocking your view of the world!"

Respecting the fears or the obligations of others is an expression of real solidarity. Have you ever thought that when so-and-so does not participate in the demonstration it might be because she has young children to look after? Or because she has some physical condition? Some members refuse tasks that involve writing — have you ever thought that it might be because they never learned how to write? Or that others may not speak up very often out of shyness?

Solidarity also means respecting a majority decision to wage a struggle, even when you are not in agreement with it. Nobody is obliged to participate in a fight in which they do not believe, but neither do they have the right to hinder those who do agree with it.

Choice of Targets

First, it is essential to choose your target well. This will allow you to concentrate your energies where they will be most effective. Taking on the State is a hazardous undertaking for a popular group, one in which victory is practically impossible. How, then, do you choose your target when you want to attack a particular policy of the State? You can do it in two ways. The first is the political way. In this case you must personalize the target (a minister, for example). ADDS applied this type of tactic when they used the slogan "Forget,[3] pay your debt!" The second way is to point the finger at a particular service.

What is important in the choice of target is that it have a direct relation to the issue being raised, and that it be accessible. In addition, the person or organization targeted must have the power to resolve the problem. In struggles whose solution can only be political it is often appropriate to go straight to the premier rather than target the person nominally in charge. In the same vein, a tenants' association is better advised to put pressure on the landlord than on the janitor. The choice of target is related to the process of research and analysis of the community. It is not always obvious who is the owner of a business or a building. By scratching the surface, you might discover that the real owner is not who you thought, or that there are several owners, one of whom is particularly vulnerable. Imagine, for example, that a part-owner of several slum apartment buildings turns out to be a politician. Obviously, his political position makes him more vulnerable, and therefore a better target, than the other owners.

Having Fun

It is important to have fun. Even though it may seem contradictory, it is possible, and even desirable, to carry on a struggle with joy. Many groups and organizations have adopted this principle. ADDS demonstrations are full of good humour and singing. Does this mean the group does not take its demands seriously? Of course not! But they understand that a collective demonstration is a happy occasion since it reaffirms solidarity. They also understand that expressing the pleasure of being together reduces the tensions involved in a struggle. People do not get involved in a fight to fulfill some need to gripe, but to express their refusal of oppression.

People hate hollow slogans, rough language, and military-style operations, but they love to sing adaptations of popular songs. The use of giant puppets, musical instruments, or even dance, can also help a group get its message across to the public humorously, and usually much more effectively. Having fun can be useful tactically.

Communications

Communication is essential in a struggle. In this section, we will look at two areas in which effective communication is particularly important: among the members of a group and with its allies, and with the media.

As we have seen, democracy in popular groups requires respect for the right of members to know everything that is going on. In periods of intense struggle, this principle must be applied even more rigorously. Among the most obvious means of informing the membership are more frequent meetings, telephone trees, newsletters, and alternative media such as community radio. These communication techniques are not exclusive to the popular movement; they are also used extensively in the union movement. During strikes, union members must meet frequently in order to find out how negotiations are going, to express their satisfaction or dissatisfaction with the progress being made by the negotiators, to take decisions on strategy and tactics, and finally to vote on the proposed labour contract.

A telephone tree can be used to reach all the members quickly. A good telephone network is an excellent weapon in the arsenal of a group in a struggle, and it encourages the involvement of members who are not available for other tasks. A newsletter is particularly good for sharing information with allies. The means chosen for internal communication will depend on a number of factors, such as the size of the membership, the scope of the struggle, and the number of allies. The basic principle, however, is always the same: reach all those who need to be informed as quickly as possible.

The use of the media, both electronic and print, fills another need, that of informing the public of the group's demands and its progress. Among the most commonly used techniques are press conferences, press releases, calls to open-line shows, and participation in public affairs programmes. While the tactic of occupying a radio or television station has sometimes been used, we will not discuss it here.

On the subject of press conferences, we will begin by stating the obvious: if you have nothing to say, don't call out the journalists; they have better things to do than listen to platitudes. But if you think what you have to say is important, then don't hesitate to call a press conference — or rather, hesitate just long enough to prepare it well. It is essential that you have solid, complete information and that your spokesperson has the best possible command of the facts. At the press conference itself, journalists who are conscientious will try to understand what interest your struggle has for an audience saturated with news. They will ask questions. It is up to you to make it clear that you are in an intolerable situation and that people must be informed of it. A few judiciously chosen examples and some clear figures will help them better understand what is at stake in your fight. It is usually a good idea to prepare a press kit containing thorough information, so that journalists can easily find enough material for articles.

A press conference requires preparation. You must find out about the deadlines for the various media, arrange the room, invite representatives of allied groups, and so on. If you invite the electronic media, make provision for separate interviews. The usual practice is to call the press conference early in the day so that the journalists can file their reports for the evening news or the next day's paper.

A press release should provide the media with information. It should be clearly written and contain new facts. It should include the name of the group issuing the release and the phone number of a spokesperson.

If the issue of your struggle comes up on an open-line programme, make sure your point of view is heard. Members of the group who phone in should be well-prepared. Remember that time is limited during an open-line show. If several persons call in, they should not all repeat the same points, but add new information or clarify what others have said.

Being a guest on a public affairs programme requires that you have a thorough knowledge of the issues. This is all the more important if you are facing a representative of the opposing party. Remember also that television transmits images, and the image of a group's representative becomes that of the whole group.

The scope of this book does not permit us to go into further detail on communications. Every organizer would be well advised to study the literature on this important subject.

Coalitions

More and more, the groups and organizations of the popular movement feel a need join forces in broader struggles. Sometimes they form coalitions with the union movement as well. Initiatives such as occupying a minister's office, organizing events like La grande marche pour l'emploi (The Big March for Jobs) and the Sommets populaires (Popular Summits) require the participation of many groups and organizations.

This kind of activity must follow a "code of ethics." First, a distinction must be made between groups that are actively involved in organizing the initiative and those groups that simply support it. It will be the actively-involved groups that decide the form and content of the action. This does not, however, prevent any other group from participating. Second, since coalitions normally include organizations of various strengths and sizes, care should be taken that the smaller groups are not submerged by the larger ones. It sometimes happens, for example, in alliances between the popular movement and the union movement that the unions, because of their large memberships and ample financial resources, are able to impose their point of view. This demonstrates a curious conception of what constitutes a democratic relationship between the two movements. Organizers should at every opportunity strive to establish an equal relationship between popular groups and unions even though it is clear from the outset that they are not of equal strength.

Finally, spokespersons for a coalition should receive their mandate from *all* the participating groups. One group should not be permitted to monopolize centre stage at the expense of the others. No group should deviate from the accepted strategy without first consulting its allies.

Evaluation

The evaluation of a collective action is as important as its planning. It is essential to assess what has been achieved in order to be better prepared for the next action. The evaluation of popular struggles, unfortunately, is often badly done, and the same errors are frequently repeated. Popular groups go through periods that are not very favourable to evaluation: times of feverish activity or times of turning inward to indulge in orgies of self-criticism leading finally to purges. Insofar as the evaluation is based on the objectives of a group, there will always be a political bias that influences the conclusions. But you must try to develop the tools to assess the situation with rigour and precision and identify possibilities for future actions. The analysis should follow certain guidelines so as not to deteriorate into political or psychological subjectivism. It should involve neither self-flagellation nor self-justification, but rather a critical analysis of all the factors affecting the attainment of the group's objectives.

Evaluations should be carried out collectively by all the participants in the struggle or action. Individuals not involved in the action can provide objective distance, but the actors must be there to provide the facts. Furthermore, since it is the active members of the group who must carry on the work, they are the ones who need to learn from the evaluation, and it should be carried out with their full participation and for their benefit. An evaluation by intellectuals who have had no part in the action would be of little value to the organization and its activists.

Many approaches have been used, and there is no magic formula. It all depends on what you want to do and the means you have to do it. Time constraints, the number of people involved and their level of education, the work schedule, the distribution of tasks, the distance from the action being evaluated, and the future needs of the organization are all factors to consider when making an evaluation. Some organizations have gotten so tangled up in evaluations that they stopped activities for months. An evaluation may be healthy and necessary, but it should not be allowed to demobilize a group. It should be of manageable scope for everyone involved, and it should be designed to provide results, at least in the medium term. That would mean not more than a few weeks or months, including several days of intense discussion involving the group as a whole. You can also make a summary evaluation in a one-day meeting with a minimum of preparation, but this may not provide any results other than readjustments during the course of an action.

An evaluation requires preparation. It should involve people who will be stimulated by the exercise regardless of whether the appraisal of the action is positive or negative. It is important that the basis for analysis be clearly defined and that everyone recognize the validity of the procedure used. Internal stresses tend to come to the surface during an evaluation, and objectivity and flexibility are needed to deal with them. A climate of openness and trust is essential, especially if there are serious political differences within the organization. You should never lose sight of the ultimate goal of the evaluation: to keep up the struggle.

Important factors in an evaluation

An evaluation is an analysis of the impact of an action in relation to both the initial objectives (these are not always well defined) and the group's current situation, internal and external. It requires the most complete description possible of context, sequence of events, and the organization targeted by the action. It will take time to put together all this information: the operation can easily be carried out collectively using a board to note the main points. The collective memory of the group will help reconstruct events.

An evaluation is best carried out in a group of at most fifteen people who have been involved throughout the struggle. More groups can be formed if a greater number of activists has been involved, but this can become complicated. Evaluations rarely involve more than the core activists and organizers. It is useful, however, to consult members who have participated in a marginal way, in order to have a different point of view and particularly to see how well the action succeeded in mobilizing people outside the core. When other groups have joined in a coalition or given their support, it is useful to have their feedback or even to have them take part in the evaluation process.

Once the facts have been established and placed in context, you must analyze them to establish the relations of cause and effect. This is where the actual evaluation takes place, and where political biases and conflicts can influence the conclusions. Depending on the interpretation of the events, different follow-ups can be proposed, all in the name of the group's best interests. When power relations and the impact of actions are being analyzed, it is easy, in spite of all efforts to be methodical, for different individuals to draw conflicting conclusions, but the more precise the analysis, the better the evaluation will be and the clearer the course of future action. It is also important to realize that evaluations are not only for the benefit of the group making them, but for the popular movement as a whole.

The analysis can be carried out by the core group making the evaluation or by a smaller committee that prepares a draft for discussion. Preliminary reports can also be submitted to a more broad-based body in the organization, such as the board of directors or even the general meeting. Workshop discussions can take place on the basis of a summary or a thorough analysis provided by the participants, leaving time for the planning of future action. These ways of proceeding are certainly quicker and less tedious, but they are also less fruitful as learning experiences. They may also be less mobilizing since the conclusions are not the product of as broad a collective effort. On other hand, the conclusions will likely be more coherent since a collective text is usually the product of compromise.

The principle of control by the members requires that they be involved as much as possible in the evaluation itself and the discussion of the future course of action. At the same time, there must be a minimum of rigour in order for the exercise to be productive. Not everyone can or wants to be involved in the whole evaluation process, but democracy requires that they be fully informed about it and participate fully in the decisions that follow from it. The results of the evaluation thus remain in the control of the members, without them being burdened with the preparation and writing of it. The most active members should take charge of the evaluation, but they must make sure they have the democratic support of the entire organization.

The Departure of the Organizer

It is important to be able to integrate into a community, but it is just as important to know how to leave. Most organizers leave the community after a few years of working with a group. This departure should be the result of a job well done, including helping the group set up appropriate structures, developing the independence of the membership, and fostering a leadership capable of taking over from the professional organizer. Another reason for organizers to leave is the need to take some distance from their work and to regain their emotional balance. Work in a context of struggle and conflict is very stressful and there is no point in going beyond your limits.

Whatever the reason for departure, it should take place gradually and as smoothly and calmly as possible. This means that the people with whom you are working should be warned well in advance so that they can get used to the idea of your absence and make the necessary changes. You very likely will have developed friendships in the community. After sharing many happy and sad events with people, you will be like a member of the family. These relations should not be broken abruptly. On the other hand, nothing is more of a drag than an organizer who refuses to leave. If you decide to leave, leave! Sometimes organizers consider it perfectly legitimate to keep on working with a group. This kind of paternalism or maternalism not only complicates the work of whoever has replaced you, but it may also undermine what you have accomplished.

It goes without saying that except in circumstances beyond their control, organizers should never drop a group in the middle of a struggle or when the group's existence is still precarious. You must respect the ethics of community organizing. Organizers who are not concerned with the consequence of their actions not only harm a community but contribute to demobilization and discredit organizers in general. This may seem obvious, but history shows that good intentions are not enough.

Celebrating Victories and Nursing Wounds

Community organizing involves victories and defeats. It is legitimate and desirable to celebrate victories. Celebrations should be organized so that everyone takes part, not just a handful of core activists. It is always painful to see a little clique having a private party at the corner bar while the rest go home bitter and disappointed. When this happens, members understandably get the feeling that they are not really part of the gang but just bodies to be gotten out when needed. Instead, rent a hall or invite all the members to the office for a party. Childcare arrangements and invitations to allies should also be considered. Everything should be done to maximize the participation of everyone who contributed to the group's success.

At the risk of sounding like incurable optimists, we will venture to say that there are no absolute defeats, any more than there are total victories. In the case of what might be considered a defeat, it is important to be able to point to minor gains, such as increased solidarity, greater public awareness of the situation you are opposing, exposure of contradictions, or development of a network of allies. In addition, it should be remembered that an apparent defeat may, in time, be turned into a victory. You should be aware that any defeat affects the morale of the troops. An organizer should be able to motivate the members and help them maintain their confidence. The activities of the popular movement continue regardless of setbacks. There is no point in rubbing salt in your wounds. Better to roll up your sleeves for the next battle in the long struggle for justice and dignity.

NOTES

1. *Rules for Radicals* (New York: Random House, 1971), pp. 127-30.

2. Translators' note: Québec public sector unions belonging to the three major labour federations in Québec formed a common front to negotiate with the government.

3. Translators' note: Claude Forget, the minister responsible for welfare at the time.

IV

HOW GROUPS FUNCTION

The work of the community organizer, as we have seen, requires a high level of skill and knowledge. We have discussed the importance of doing research and understanding the community as preconditions for any organizing effort. In the section on struggle, we emphasized the need for planning, and for as much control as possible by the group's membership. In the last part of the book, we will deal chiefly with the internal functioning of groups and with working methods that aim to prevent participation from deteriorating into chaos. We will also discuss such difficult questions as the eventual dissolution of a group and the problem of funding.

Seven

INTERNAL DEMOCRACY

A Place for Everyone and Everyone in Their Place

Nothing is worse for a group than a division of labour that puts the bulk of the workload on a few members. This is harmful in two ways: the members who are doing all the work will quickly burn out; and the members who don't have enough to do will lose interest in the group. Distribution of tasks is one of the most important aspects of building a group that functions well and has a true sense of solidarity. Training is key, because it enables members to acquire skills and prepares them to take on tasks related to organizing, accounting, information, or leadership, functions that are essential to any group. Unlike State institutions, popular groups cannot depend on experts. Members feel involved in the group by performing tasks that suit their abilities and that are useful. You should avoid the kind of approach, however, that claims it is enough to belong to the working class or an oppressed group to automatically be able to do something. There is nothing bourgeois about making sure members are capable of carrying out the functions they take on. It simply saves them needless criticism. Training and distributing tasks go hand in hand, and both are essential to group democracy.

There Are No Unimportant Tasks

No one will deny that being a spokesperson for a group — seeing yourself on television, hearing yourself on the radio, standing side by side with union leaders on a platform — makes you feel important. Speaking for a group sometimes serves as preparation for a political career. In some groups, this "plum" job is monopolized by one or two knowledgeable paid staff. Spokespersons, however, are nothing without the work of the membership.

Women often claim that there is a tendency in groups to give them the tasks that men avoid, such as addressing envelopes, cleaning, and preparing food. This criticism is legitimate, and while some progress has been made, in general the situation in mixed groups has been slow to change.

These examples show that, in popular groups as elsewhere, not all tasks are equally valued. Organizers should help the members make sure they don't reproduce the inequalities of class society in their group, and promote the idea that no task is unimportant. There's no law that says a university graduate can't do dishes or that a working-class woman can't represent the group in a meeting with the local M.P. or union representatives.

In strictly tactical terms, a group involved in a struggle should always have several people capable of representing it on any given issue. This creates an image of a serious, well-organized group whose members know what they are talking about. A group should also take into account its own social makeup and that of the community whose interests it is defending in its choice of spokespersons. A group defending the rights of welfare recipients should be represented by welfare recipients. A youth organization should be led and represented by the young people who make it up. Anyone who thinks this position is undemocratic should take a close look at the makeup of the Québec National Assembly, the House of Commons, Chambers of Commerce, and other bodies that serve the interests of the dominant classes.

Tasks should never be delegated on the basis of sex, age, or arbitrary judgement of a member's intellectual abilities. They should be assigned by democratic choice, with the emphasis always on validation of members' abilities. This may mean that some who feel they are destined for high places will find themselves given humbler, but none-theless equally important tasks.

Solidarity

Although the word "solidarity" has fallen into disrepute, the fact remains that the level of solidarity in a group is a clear indication of its health. When a group lacks solidarity, it is usually on its last legs. Never underestimate the importance of solidarity.

Popular groups are made up of individuals who have chosen to combine their power by joining together in a common struggle. Some-times groups put aside their ideological differences to unite in broad-based organizations capable of exerting real power. Solidarity and democracy go hand in hand. They determine how popular groups operate, and give the movement credibility.

Solidarity is expressed in the many and varied ways that people demonstrate their commitment to the group. It is shown by staff members who continue to work even when the group no longer has the money to pay their salaries. It is shown in the members' participa-tion in general meetings and working committees, and in the support they give each other in times of need. Solidarity means sensitivity to others, to the realities of their lives and their level of consciousness.

Groups have been at the brink of collapse because some of their members indulged in manipulation, sectarianism, and other forms of politically immature behaviour, all the while waving the flag of solidarity at every opportunity. We would ask, solidarity with whom? The police understand the importance of solidarity. When they want to destabilize a group, they try to destroy its internal solidarity through manipulation, infiltration, and blackmail. Those who defend the State know that the more the members of a group are divided, the weaker the group becomes.

"Petty Tyrants"

Every group has had at least one member who might be called a "petty tyrant." Usually, these types do no serious harm to the group, since the members tend to avoid giving them the opportunity to exercise their unhealthy thirst for power. Petty tyrants try to get close to those they think have power. In meetings they tend to speak a lot and try to tell others what to do. Sooner or later, they are put in their place by the other members. In some cases, however, an organizer may have to take firm action against an individual who shows contempt for the membership and the rules of the group by trying to usurp power and authority. Expulsion from the group may even be necessary. We feel, however, that the petty tyrant, like any other member, should be treated with sympathy and sensitivity. A "one-on-one" meeting is usually enough to settle the problem.

Criticism and Self-criticism

Most people are afraid of criticism, particularly self-criticism. However, if made properly, criticism is a learning experience, and admitting a mistake is no catastrophe if you know the group will be understanding and ready to help repair any damage. Criticism and self-criticism are essential to the evaluation of any action. Members of popular groups are often hesitant to criticize for fear of hurting someone; they are, for the most part, generous people, but this natural generosity can lead to overpermissiveness. Experienced organizers should train members in the art of criticism. Remember that if criticism doesn't come out in meetings, it will be expressed elsewhere, and it is unhealthy for members to talk behind the backs of other members. Lack of criticism, or criticism that is not open and constructive, can undermine solidarity and lead to the breakup of the group.

Contrary to what many believe, self-criticism has nothing to do with group therapy. The point is not to "spill your guts," but rather to evaluate a group effort and the role played by each member. Being able to admit a mistake or recognize you were wrong about something is a sign of maturity. Self-criticism can help solidify the group by nipping in the bud any ill feelings among members. It is always better to hear "at least, you can admit your mistakes..." than to be accused of having a closed mind.

Self-criticism is pointless without an attempt to correct the problem. The mistake may have been due to lack of experience or knowledge, it may have been the result of personal problems, or it may be an indication of internal communication problems. One thing is certain: members who have the courage to admit their errors should never be expelled; they should be supported by the group, for the benefit of the group as a whole.

Eight

GROUP FACILITATION; STRUCTURES

Facilitating a group is an art, the art of awakening group consciousness in each of the individuals involved in the pursuit of a common goal. Although it draws on an individual's personal resources, it is based on principles and skills that can be learned. In addition, each group has its own dynamics, and a facilitator who is sensitive to this will respect the uniqueness of the group rather than follow any rigid method. The ideas presented below are intended to help inexperienced facilitators find their own methods and techniques.

Group Process

There are three levels of group process, each of which requires the use of specific techniques by the facilitator: the content level, the procedural level, and the feeling level.

The content level

In a task-oriented group or a discussion group, it is the common objective that serves as the catalyst and makes for group cohesion. Ideas and opinions exchanged among members are of prime importance. It is essential that ideas circulate freely and that the participants understand each others' views. The facilitator should be attentive to this aspect of group dynamics, making sure that information flows freely and that all the members feel they are being heard.

The procedural level

For ideas to flow freely in a group, it is important that the rules for discussion and decision-making be clearly defined and accepted by all members. Facilitators should make sure that procedural questions are dealt with, either by making their own suggestions or by asking the members to establish rules. In all instances, they must ensure that information flows freely.

The feeling level

When a number of people come together to work toward a common objective, tensions and minor conflicts inevitably occur. Sometimes emotions become so charged over differences in points of view that the group is paralyzed. The role of the facilitator is to see that a climate favorable to discussion is maintained. This can be done by encouraging the participants to express their feelings regarding the functioning of the group and the other participants.

Very often facilitators falter because they fail to take into account one of these three levels. Sometimes they make the error of systematically declaring out of order any subject not on the agenda. A facilitator's skill can be measured in his or her ability to follow the group on all three levels of process, keeping the information circulating and maintaining a balance between efficiency and interpersonal relations.

Speaking of feelings...

Staff members and resource persons in groups can work tirelessly setting up structures, raising money, and organizing meetings. Everything may be going fine when, all of a sudden, there is a flood of resignations, or perhaps the work that the group had decided to carry out is not being done. What happened? Everything was done democratically, and the group's goals correspond to the objective interests of the members. Very likely there has been an interpersonal conflict of some sort.

For many of us, the realm of feelings is as hidden as the dark side of the moon. We realize that it is important, but we don't know what to do about it. Emotional life has a great deal to do with interpersonal relationships, and the emotional life of the group affects and is affected by that of the individual. Problems in the group cause people to feel guilty and turn inward. Resistance to dealing with these problems can take many forms, such as accusations of psychologism, claims that all the group needs is to ignore its differences and work together, or arguments that the strongest and the fittest will naturally take the lead.

Rather than discuss authenticity, consistency, esteem for other people, and other attitudes usually viewed by specialists as fundamental to our emotional lives, we will ask, instead, why people join groups and what kind of relations they seek. We know they join popular groups primarily to fill certain needs, such as the need for human contact, for information, for help with a problem, for a specific service, or for material benefit. If these primary needs are met, some individuals will want to take part in the collective process of the group. They will become the activists. Relationships with the other members will develop as he or she becomes integrated. That is why every group should have mechanisms for making new members feel welcome and fostering their participation.

As we have emphasized throughout this book, the individual is of prime importance. Groups are strengthened when all members feel that they are important and that their contributions are valued. The quality of interpersonal relations depends on a number of factors, some of them quite subtle. Organizers should get to know the individuals with whom they are working. They should appreciate the personal situation of each member and take it into account in their dealings with that person. For example, they should not expect the same involvement from a member who has young children at home or a full-time job as from one who has fewer responsibilities. Members' health should also be considered; you don't drag people with heart conditions to certain kinds of demonstrations, for example, but you can ask them to take on support tasks. Similarly, you should respect the fact that some people are shy or have trouble speaking, and you should never place people in situations where they may be humiliated or have their self-confidence destroyed.

Sometimes you must have the courage to speak frankly. You should also be willing to admit your own mistakes. You don't have to be close friends with everyone, but to build solidarity you must be aware of the importance of feelings as a source of conflict or strength in the group. Organizations have had major internal problems because of leaders who reached a point where they could no longer function emotionally. Such painful situations are bad for the movement and we must learn to avoid them.

Facilitation Techniques

There are simple techniques to help the facilitator deal with problems that occur at each of the three levels of process: clarification techniques for the content level, control techniques for the procedural level, and techniques for the feeling level.

Clarification

Defining. Since the group has come together for a common purpose, it is important for the facilitator to make sure at the beginning that that purpose has been clearly defined. If it has not, take the time required to do so. Similarly, the vocabulary used by the participants is often imprecise and ambiguous. The facilitator should constantly make sure that the words being used mean the same things for all the members of the group. If necessary, ask the participants to define their terms.

Reformulating. A good way to keep information flowing is to occasionally reformulate what a participant says, especially if others seem not to have understood. This technique is particularly effective in making the participants aware of communication problems and developing group consciousness. It also helps increase their ability to listen. Finally, it helps the participant who has spoken to think about what he or she has said and to clarify it if necessary.

Making connections. One of the difficulties in teamwork is that participants do not pay enough attention to what others bring to the group. The facilitator can help with this problem by asking the person who has spoken to make the connection with what was said before. You can also point out connections you see that have not been made explicit by the participants. This encourages people to listen more closely and tends to focus the discussion.

Summarizing. From time to time the facilitator can let the participants take a breather by summing up for them the various opinions that have been expressed. You may also make a synthesis of them or ask the group to do so. If the group has chosen a secretary, he or she can also occasionally summarize what has been recorded. This permits the group to take stock or to change the direction of the discussion if necessary.

Control

Encouraging participation. In any group there are some participants who don't talk much and some who say nothing. Facilitators should not feel they have to make everyone talk, but they should promote the participation of the silent ones. The method of systematically going around the table and having everyone speak in turn is not advisable since it creates pressure and makes it even more painful for the timid. The best way to get a member to take part is to wait for a moment when he or she seems more at ease and less self-conscious, then ask for his or her opinion. It is often when discussion is liveliest that these opportunities occur, and an attentive facilitator can make sure that those who speak the least get the first chance.

Curbing. Every group also has participants who speak easily, at length, and often. The task of the facilitator is to curb such individuals and help them learn restraint. This will be easier if the facilitator has a good relationship with them, and if it can be done with humour, so much the better. Just summarizing what they have said and asking others to give their opinions may be enough to limit their input. You can also ask them to summarize for themselves, and challenge them to do it in less than five sentences.

Timekeeping. In order to avoid wasting time on details and to speed up the discussion, the facilitator can occasionally remind the group how much time is left. You can also ask the group at the beginning to estimate how much time should be spent on each item of the agenda; if necessary, the group can be asked to modify the agenda.

Giving the floor. Usually the facilitator is expected to give each speaker the floor in turn. This can be done formally for all speakers, or only for those who prefer it. Participants can also be allowed to speak without having to ask for the floor. What is important is that you clarify the procedure to be used and change it according to the needs of the group. In any case, the facilitator retains the right to speak at any time and can use that right to bring the meeting to order, if necessary.

Dealing with feelings

Welcoming. The facilitator can encourage participation by warmly welcoming each participant. Greeting each person individually, no matter what their status, also helps validate them in the group.

Dispelling tension. The facilitator can foster solidarity by letting the participants relax and joke among themselves from time to time. Breaks in the discussion help dispel tension and fatigue and make the work of the group easier.

Being objective. If an emotionally charged conflict arises between two of the participants, the facilitator can ease tensions by reformulating the issue in an objective manner, and thus help participants avoid getting blocked by personality conflicts.

Verbalizing. When a tense atmosphere has developed for no apparent reason, it may be helpful to encourage the participants to verbalize what they are feeling. Likewise, when you are facing a problem that seems insurmountable, it may be useful to verbalize what you are feeling. Once a feeling is put into words, it is much easier to deal with.

A skilled facilitator is aware of all three levels of process, whatever the techniques he or she uses. If some techniques are difficult for you, other participants can be asked to use them. A good way of learning to facilitate is to record a meeting, then note later how you respond on the three levels.

Structures

How to avoid "meeting-itis"

The effectivness of an organization is not directly proportional to the number of meetings it holds. In fact, in our experience, holding lots of meetings is often a way for a group to hide its ineffectiveness. "Meeting-itis" is an ailment that can wear members out and cause them to lose interest in the group and its activities.

Democracy requires that the members of a group be constantly involved in the decision-making process, but it also means taking into account the limits on their availability. Working-class culture emphasizes the practical, and ordinary working people are not particularly drawn to the long discussions so dear to intellectuals. Meetings provide a justification for the salaries of those who earn their living as community organizers, but for most members they are an extra chore added on to an eight-hour work day in the factory or office. For most women, meetings are added to their double workload as housewives and salaried workers. Meetings should never be called unnecessarily. Avoiding "meeting-itis" demonstrates a concern for democracy since it prevents decision-making from being monopolized by a handful of members who have more time for meetings.

Committees

Committees are not only excellent for getting work done; they are also the best way to integrate and train members. This cannot be repeated too often!

Usually, committees are struck by means of a motion passed at a general meeting. This is particularly true with permanent committees such as information, finance, education, and strategy committees. This type of committee is generally chaired by a member of the board of directors, who reports to the board on the work of the committee.

It is often better if the chair of a committee is elected. In this way the members of the board can be chosen according to their interests and their skills. Sometimes the board can create an ad hoc committee to carry out a specific task. This type of committee has a limited mandate and is set up for a limited period of time. Ad hoc committees might be set up to organize a social event or a fund-raising activity, to study a particular issue, or to analyse some unforeseen event.

Whatever the type, committees are really the heart of a group, the essence of its internal functioning, its struggles, and its activities.

There are several reasons why committees make good training grounds for members. There is more opportunity for expression on committees than in other activities because of the smaller numbers of people involved. As well, those who join a committee usually know more about the subject concerned. If there are no "experts " in the group, it is always possible to call upon resource persons.

Whether they come from within or outside the group, it is important that resource persons asked to take part in a committee be aware of their educational role. Members should be able increase their knowledge through their contact with "experts." At the same time, the experts can also benefit from the knowledge and experience of the committee members.

The results of the work of committees are usually passed on to the board of directors, which uses them to make decisions regarding the group's activities. Unlike the government, the popular movement does not have the means to set up committees whose reports will simply be shelved. The work of committees is important, and members must take their role seriously and fulfill their mandate in the time allotted.

The executive

The executive is generally chosen from among the members of the board following the general meeting at which the board was elected. It usually consists of four members: president, vice-president, secretary, and treasurer. Its composition can be changed by the members, but these four functions are essential. It may also be a good idea to have the executive elected directly by the entire membership at a general meeting or convention.

It goes without saying that members who agree to sit on the executive must be capable of doing the job. This means being well acquainted with the goals and activities of the group, having time to take part in frequent meetings, and having a strong sense of solidarity with the other members of the executive. There is an unwritten law that decisions of the executive be made by consensus; this demands greater-than-average political maturity.

The executive committee plays a key role. It is responsible for the operations of the organization between meetings of the board of directors, and it prepares the agenda for board meetings. The members of the executive are the natural spokespersons for the group in dealings with other groups and funding organizations. They will also be the best informed, since all information will necessarily pass through their hands.

The special status of the members of the executive requires that they take care not to form an authoritarian clique. They are the guardians of the democratic rights of the membership and they will fulfill their mandate more effectively if they have the support of the majority of members.

The makeup of the executive should also reflect that of the group. There should be adequate representation of women. Generally speaking, there should not be more petty-bourgeois members than members representative of the local community or the social class for which the group claims to be fighting. Meetings of the executive are usually set by collective decision, and the president or the staff of the organization sees that the other members receive the agenda several days ahead of time.

The board of directors

The board of directors is the highest authority between conventions or general meetings of the membership. Its meetings are set by its members at the preceding meeting. Meetings of the board can also be called by the executive if the business of the group requires it. Usually the organization's secretary or the staff sends board members the agenda a few days before the meeting. Members of the board are elected democratically by secret ballot at a general meeting of the membership. They can also be named to the board to replace a member who resigns.

Being elected to the board is an indication of the confidence of the membership, but it also involves giving more time than others. If you are nominated for election to the board of directors, you should be prepared to say no if you do not have the time and energy required by the job. People can be so impressed by the honour of the nomination that they forget about the responsibilities it entails. Such individuals are likely to make poor board members and harm the functioning of the group.

Each board member should not only be well informed about the group's activities as a whole, but have a specific area of responsibility. This may seem obvious, but groups sometimes pack their boards with "important people" in a mistaken attempt to "give the group credibility." The popular movement is not the place for people who merely want to lend their names to a "good cause" and relieve their consciences by formally participating in the administration of groups that work with people who would otherwise be foreign to them. Avoid the temptation to give a group false credibility through "honorary appointments" of such individuals.

Meetings of the board of directors should be carefully prepared so that the items on the agenda can be seriously discussed and decisions made. Agendas that are poorly planned or too heavy can prevent board members from doing their work properly.

Childcare should be provided for board members by other members of the group. Everything should be done to allow every member to participate in the group's activities, and this includes ensuring that personal responsibilities do not prevent anyone from taking part in decision-making. Women have legitimately criticized the anti-democratic functioning of groups with regard to women members. These criticisms should be acted on.

The general meeting

Popular groups usually hold an annual general meeting of the membership, called by the board, so that the members can take stock of the group's achievements over the past year. The general meeting is the highest decision-making body, and no other level of the organization can revoke its decisions. General meetings should be prepared with the utmost care and everything possible done to enable members to participate fully in the decisions that will determine the course of the group for the coming year.

The general meeting is usually chaired by the president until there is an election of the new board. The members then choose a president of elections who sees that the new board of directors is elected according to democratic procedures.

The board should prepare for the general meeting by setting up an organizing committee, allocating a budget, and deciding on the form of the meeting — for example, whether there will be workshops, whether to have discussion leaders from outside the group, if meals will be provided. The board should decide on the list of subjects to be discussed and draft any motions to be presented, such as changes to the group's charter or bylaws, proposals for new programmes and activities, and financial statements and budget. They should also include any business brought up by members in accordance with the bylaws, the official acceptance of new members, and, if need be, the expulsion of others.

The organizing committee carries out the board's decisions. It organizes preliminary meetings, sets up childcare services or makes arrangements with a daycare centre, meets with workshop leaders, and prepares information to be sent to the members so that they can familiarize themselves with it before the meeting. The organizing committee should also make arrangements for billeting, meals, and a social evening, as required. To carry out all these tasks, the organizing committee sets up subcommittees and coordinates their activities.

There is one cardinal rule for general meetings: aim for the participation of every member. This will often mean calling on individuals from outside the group to lead workshops, operate audio-visual equipment, or provide childcare and meals. These should be people involved in the popular movement or the union movement, and preferably already familiar with your group and its activities.

These rules do not necessarily apply to all groups. A general meeting of a large organization is more complicated to prepare than one for a tenants' association with twenty members. Modifications should be made according to the number of members, whether the organization is local, regional, or national, and the type of meeting you wish to hold.

A general meeting usually starts and ends with a presentation by the president. The members are then asked to adopt the agenda and the minutes of the last general meeting. Some items on the agenda are optional, while others are obligatory. The latter include the financial report, budget, membership fees, evaluation of the activities, election of the board, and any special motions, such as an appeal of the expulsion of a member.

A general meeting is not a convention or a conference. It is an administrative body that decides the direction and activities of the group. It is sometimes preferable to break it up into two meetings, with one for strictly administrative matters, including elections, and the other to discuss topics related to the activities and struggles of the group. The important thing is that the members be able to make decisions without being rushed, taking the time to think about the questions before them and to raise questions of their own.

The social part of a general meeting is important. In many groups, all the members rarely have a chance to get together. The social activities should let them get better acquainted while unwinding after a long day of discussion and decision-making. Some groups call on the members to take an active part in these evenings by putting on sketches, singing, reciting poetry, or playing music. This validates "people's culture" and builds solidarity among members.

The bylaws of most structured groups include provisions for holding special general meetings. These meetings are normally called by the board of directors, but they can also be called by a certain number of members in good standing. The latter procedure should not be abused or the membership will get fed up. You should not hesitate to call a special general meeting, however, if there is a serious threat to the interests of the group.

Nine

FUNDING GROUPS
DISSOLUTION

Popular organizations and the working class in general have been the first to suffer the consequences of the current economic situation. Budget cuts at various levels of government have had a serious effect on funding for groups. Most are in precarious financial circumstances, and many face the prospect of demise. Though economic hard times mean that popular groups are needed more than ever, what has occurred is a certain degree of demobilization and burn-out. Groups find themselves facing the dilemma of whether to allow themselves to be coopted by governments who want to maintain the image of social democracy, or to fight to maintain their political autonomy while looking to the State and other sources for funding.

The problem of funding has always taken up a lot of time and energy, and has been the cause of many internal crises, sometimes resulting in the demise of groups. In this chapter, we will examine the financial problems of popular groups, then look at the question of self-financing, and, finally, offer some suggestions regarding funding and grants.

Problems Created by the Economic Situation

The funding of popular groups has always been shaky, but they have managed to get by through government programmes and fund-raising campaigns. Outside funding has encouraged a "grant mentality," a dependent attitude that has led to internal problems and sometimes dissolution. This is aggravated by amateurish management of funds and inadequate financial planning. In the area of self-financing, the popular movement has shown little imagination.

In some organizations, although there is an individual or a committee in charge of fund-raising, the problem does not stimulate much interest. When there are cutbacks or termination of government programmes, there is a hue and cry, but the protest is always related to maintaining acquired rights. Some of these problems are related to low membership. The groups most able to defend themselves against cuts are those with structures that enable members to respond to the crisis by making their voices heard, deciding on actions and collectively maintaining the functioning of the organization. This is not the case for groups that rely on one or two paid staff and a few core members. When things get rough and the paid people must find other jobs, the members do not have the support they need to fight.[1] The worsening economic situation is an important external factor in groups' financial problems, but there are also internal factors related to how they operate.

Let us start by looking at some of the external factors that result in cuts. At a fall 1979 regional meeting of voluntary groups working in popular education, four major reasons were identified for the cuts in grants to groups.

First, the criteria are becoming narrower, putting grants beyond the reach of certain groups. For example, the requirement of a charity number excludes groups involved in activities of a political nature, because such groups cannot obtain official recognition as charities.

Second, increasingly complicated requirements regarding administration and control cause problems for groups that are not so tightly administered. The obligation to supply reports, balance sheets, and programme objectives scares some groups away from even applying. This type of control also leads to self-censorship, causing groups to concentrate more and more on providing services, and to do less and less in the way of protest and mobilization. Groups become bureaucratic and their original energy is stifled. Some say that giving a group a big grant is the best way to kill it, because it makes the group dependent on the funding body and mires it in administrative and political constraints, and because it tends to make the staff focus on applying for and keeping up grants in order to justify their jobs.

A third factor in cutbacks is arbitrary decisions by government bureaucrats or funding organizations to change their priorities or reinterpret their criteria for funding. When this occurs, groups often try to fight the changes, but usually with little success.

Finally, the fourth factor leading to cuts in grants is government decisions to take over the services offered. This tactic is used less in recent years, now that the government is cutting back whole areas of services.

In addition to these external factors, there are also internal factors. We have already mentioned the lack of a sufficient base for mobilization, and inadequate planning and lack of rigour in administration. Careless accounting or insufficient controls on spending are unforgivable. No organization can afford not to have its books in order and up to date. Not only does the democratic functioning of an organization demand that information be accessible to the membership, but groups must be above suspicion in the eyes of funding organizations and government authorities. There are enough political reasons for governments to cut support without groups giving them the excuse of poor financial management. Political correctness does not excuse administrative incompetence.

Another important principle is sharing the burden of concern for the group's financial well-being among the staff and members. Everyone should be constantly concerned with the question of survival and with methods and sources of funding, though not everyone has to take part in the bookkeeping and day-to-day control of expenses. A well-run organization does not require that everyone know how to do everything, but it does require openness in administration so that no one can monopolize control. Responsibility for the control of expenses and revenues must be shared. The general meeting and the board should make the major financial decisions and see that they are carried out. Day-to-day accounting operations should be accessible so that the membership has ultimate control over finances.

Groups can avoid serious problems by sharing responsibility for fund-raising among the paid staff and the members. The members can contribute by organizing self-financing activities such as benefit evenings, sales of literature and buttons, and appeals for contributions. They can also work on grant applications and take part in negotiations with funding organizations. The interests and capabilities of the members should be taken into account and their knowledge and contacts used to the best advantage in assigning these tasks.

The precarious financial situation of groups raises questions not only about self-financing, but about how groups operate in general. Should they depend so much on paid staff? Should they adamantly refuse to ask for payment for services and literature? Discussion of these issues has begun in the last few years, and groups have started to provide fewer free services. But no one has considered asking the most financially deprived of the population to pay for services. The issue of the relation to the State is particularly thorny. Should groups go on trying to maintain and increase funding from the State at the risk of losing their autonomy, or should they work towards self-financing? These options are not mutually exclusive, and each has advantages and risks.

The biggest problems with funding by the State are its instability and the administrative and political controls attached to it. The advantage of State funding is that it can provide an office and staff, but they come with strings attached. There is always a danger of loss of autonomy or cooptation, or, at best, self-censorship and decreased activism. Financial dependence leads to political dependence, as when groups are obliged to design their activities according to grant programmes. They are then at the mercy of government policies.

Self-financing is equally precarious, but it eliminates the danger of self-censorship. It also forces groups to stay in tune with the interests of their target populations, thus favouring mobilization. We will look at the constraints and advantages of self-financing in more detail later, but we stress that State funding and self-financing can be complementary. It is a matter of choosing the grants and the forms of self-financing that offer the most advantages to the group.

Self-financing

Not only does it affect relations with the State, but self-financing also affects the orientation and operation of a group. All popular groups should, like unions, aim for financial independence. That means providing for their needs through membership fees, revenue from services or the sale of publications, and fund-raising activities. Self-financing means, above all, not relying on grants, and particularly not being dependent on funding organizations whose political goals are very different from those of the group. The politics of a group should be those of the members and the people who contribute to it. This dependence on the masses is not always easy, as some union leaders have found, but it is the most healthy, democratic way in which to operate. It gives groups the freedom they need to criticize institutions and governments. They can still take advantage of occasional grants to supplement their regular budgets, but their normal operations will not be jeopardized if a grant is lost.

But is self-financing a realistic option for popular groups, which work with low-income populations and provide non-profit social services? Only with drastic reductions in infrastructure. All groups, however, should develop self-financing activities. The "solidarity fund" of nine popular groups in Québec City is a good example of solidarity in self-financing. The fund was set up to fill the gap left when Québec City Centraide (United Way) cut funding to several groups, and its goal is to provide fifty to sixty per cent of funding. There are also regional coordinating committees in Montréal, the Ottawa Valley, and the Eastern Townships. These are initiatives on which the popular movement should build.

There are many advantages to self-financing:

-It is a barometer of the members' commitment and the community's support.
-It provides opportunities for general mobilization.
-It stimulates creativity and imagination.
-It provides a learning experience for the members.
-It fosters team spirit and group cohesion.
-It builds solidarity among groups.

-It presents an opportunity for the group to reaffirm and
publicize its goals.
-It brings funding with "no strings attached."
-It reduces dependence on traditional funding sources.
-It increases dependence on the membership and the community,
thus fostering democracy and encouraging clearly defined
goals.
-It can bring new members and activists into the group.

Fund-raising campaigns are good for motivation and mobilization.
They force old activists to talk about the goals they take for granted. They
can be a good remedy for bureaucratization. The possibilities for fund-
raising are unlimited, but whatever activity is chosen, it should be a means
of attaining the financial and publicity objectives. It should also be fun,
not require too much investment of time and money, and involve as many
members as possible in tasks that suit their skills.

A benefit evening can be an opportunity for less active members
to show their musical or decorating talents. An information table can
be a chance to meet people and learn to talk about the activities of the
group. Direct mail appeals for funds can be handled by a "work party"
that spends a few hours addressing, collating, stapling, folding, stuff-
ing, and stamping envelopes. A fund-raising activity can provide an
opportunity to renew old links or create new ones with other popular
groups. Fund-raising can be combined with the launching of a publication or the première of a film or a play. Self-financing activities can
be of benefit politically and organizationally as well as financially — if
you know how to plan them.

Applying for Funding

First establish your aims, your programme of action, and therefore your needs. Then draw up a list of potential sources of revenue.
Too many groups define their programmes according to the funding
available and lose sight of their original goals.

Priorities for funding sources should be established, based on the
energy required, the chances of success, and the political and ad-

ministrative constraints involved. Groups can achieve some stability in funding when they deal with funding organizations whose application forms don't change from year to year, especially if their political criteria are compatible with the aims of the group. You can easily re-apply year after year with assured success. Centraide used to be such a funding source. Many government ministries, on the other hand, regularly create new programmes with very heavy political and administrative requirements. An example is the various job creation programmes of the Seventies and Eighties, which have often resulted in dependency and demobilization of groups.

Aim to diversify your sources of funding. This is a principle that is respected more out of necessity than by political design. When a group has a stable source of major funding, it tends to take things easy — until the funding body changes its policies or decides that the group no longer fits its criteria. This is what happened when Centraide cut off several groups. There are no guarantees, and it is best to avoid dependence on a single source, even if this is difficult. The political autonomy of the group is enhanced when each funding body finances only part of its activities and therefore cannot control the group.

Keeping track of deadlines for various grant applications is essential for a group that wants to have several sources of funding. Take the time to prepare applications properly rather than do them at the last minute. Looking at a year at a time allows you to see funding possibilities as a whole, and to make informal inquiries and prepare applications in advance.

One last principle to keep in mind is that of honest opportunism. This may seem like a contradiction in terms, but it is not really. Opportunism consists in taking advantage of easy funding opportunities whenever they arise. This requires imagination and sometimes means not being overly purist. Groups have often boycotted federal funding sources for political reasons; instead, they should have used them and even played off the federal and provincial governments against each other. A group can make some political concessions that do not affect its overall programme without becoming a stooge of a government.

You should be honest in your dealings with funding sources. Providing false information could threaten the survival of your group and damage the credibility of the popular movement. Falsified documents or reports could lead to litigation or be used to discredit your group. Every time a popular group is criticized, other groups suffer the consequences. Honesty does not require telling all, or painting a negative portrait of the group, but it does mean not exaggerating your accomplishments. In the long term, honesty will lead to better relations with funding organizations and will strengthen your group's autonomy.

It is important to distinguish the various sources of funding for groups. There are government programmes, parapublic organizations such as Centraide, private foundations like Ford and Donner, religious institutions such as the Conference of Bishops and Plura, and financial institutions — banks, credit unions, and business.

Government programmes and parapublic organizations usually have application forms, publicly available criteria, and deadlines; these dictate how applications should be presented. The other sources require more imagination and more discipline because you have to put together the application yourself. The guiding principles for these applications should be clarity, precision, and conciseness. Always put yourself in the place of the person who has to read many applications and must find out quickly what organization is making the application, its goals, how it operates, and its activities; who the project is for; what the group wants to do and why; how it plans to do it, including the timetable; and how much the group is requesting and its budget. We will not dwell on technical details here, but rather on the relations between funding organizations and groups, and the fund-raising strategies that should be developed.

Any grant application should emphasize those aspects of the project that will interest the funding organization. If there are many facets to the project and you are applying to several organizations to help fund it, a covering letter should outline the aspects of the project that are particularly relevant for the particular funding organization. You should therefore be well informed about the orientations of each potential funding source.

A personal meeting can help clarify information in the application or correct misconceptions about the group. Whether you are dealing with government or a private organization, an approach that is polite, diplomatic, and firm can further your application. Personal contact can make your project stand out from a mass of anonymous proposals, and help you understand the requirements and priorities of the funding body. Good relations with the funding organization can also be helpful in guiding your application through the selection process and its presentation to a selection committee.

If you are able to arrange a meeting with the funding body, a delegation should be formed of no more than two or three persons, depending on the formality of the meeting. This delegation should include someone who has been empowered to answer technical questions on the finances of the group and the project, someone who has a thorough knowledge of the activities of the group and its development over the last few years, and a representative of the activity or project being proposed. The delegation will usually be made up of a paid staff person and at least one democratically elected representative, always important for credibility. It may also be useful to have a user of the group's programme in order to demonstrate the mobilization and involvement of the target population. Care should be taken to plan the role of each delegate. The more delegates there are, the greater the danger they will contradict one another. Role-playing beforehand can be useful in defining the roles: principal spokesperson, technical expert, project user.

Links with funding sources should be maintained by means of reports or mailings, as well as letters of thanks. You can also ask to be informed of any changes in funding policy. Reasons can be found to maintain contact throughout the year, promoting good relations while maintaining the autonomy of the group. If the requirements of the funding outweigh the advantages, priorities and methods can be adjusted accordingly.

Evaluation

Finally, we must emphasise the importance of keeping files on all fund-raising activities. A frequent problem with groups is their lack of collective memory and continuity. Complete files on funding sources, their technical and political requirements, contacts, methods of application, and chances of success, as well as information on methods of self-financing, should be kept in one place, so that the group is not forced to continually repeat the same futile steps. This information should be updated so that applications can be adjusted accordingly.

For example, the evaluation of a benefit evening is important in order to avoid repeating errors. Information should include the time required for printing flyers, posters, and tickets, procedures for renting the hall and obtaining a liquor permit, and contracts with suppliers. Keeping complete information can be valuable in simplifying the work of a group and demystifying its activities. In addition, you should take advantage of the experience of similar groups by finding out about methods they have used. We learn from our mistakes and the mistakes of others.

Dissolution of a Group

Some groups are very short-lived. How long a group lasts depends on what brought it together and, to a large extent, the stability of its funding. With the arrival of State funding, particularly from the federal government, groups appear and disappear with the whims of politicians and technocrats. Even projects with solid funding cease activities because of general lack of interest. This was the case with several tenants' associations and some food coops.

What, then, remains of all the effort people put into setting up groups to defend their rights and provide services? Basically two things are left: experience and materials. The experience should be available somewhere; it is always useful for others to know what pitfalls await them. It is a good idea for the members of a group that dissolves to leave their records with an organization like the Centre populaire de documentation (Popular Resource Centre), the Centre de formation populaire (Popular Training Centre), or an organization still active in the field. Materials and furniture can also be passed on.

A group may dissolve in order to merge with another, stronger organization, although this does not happen often. A dissolution for this reason would have to take place with the free consent of the members, and have been seriously studied beforehand. We do not intend to discuss dissolutions that take place for political reasons; there is no point in opening old wounds. We do believe, however, that the painful experience of the latter half of the Seventies should not be forgotten. Popular groups must not be dissolved on the false premise that their activities are reformist and that they are obstacles to major socio-political change.

The combined strength of the popular movement and the union movement may not be enough to bring about radical social change, but it can provide a basis for such change. These two movements, representing the interests of the exploited and oppressed majority, are the focal points of resistance and struggle. They have contributed greatly to the development of modern Québec, and in the current economic and political context they face even greater challenges.

NOTES

1. This was pointed out by Marcel Artaud in "Le financement des groupes populaires. Le commerce des idées doit-il être déficitaire?" in *Le Temps fou*, No. 12 (Dec. 1980), p. 43.

CONCLUSION

It may be useful at this point to sum up what we have attempted to do in this book. First we presented a brief history of popular groups in Québec so that community organizers can gain some sense of the many struggles that have taken place over the last two decades and possibly use this experience in their own work. We then looked at the people involved in community organizing, the interest groups with whom they work, and the communities and organizations in which they work.

Although an aura of romanticism often surrounds the figure of the community organizer, it should be remembered that there is nothing mystical about community organizing; it can be studied and learned like any other occupation. It involves skills, techniques, and methods that have been tested by thousands of organizers in a variety of settings and with varying degrees of success. Community organizing requires more than good will. A genuine desire to do useful work implies a willingness to do the necessary research and analysis. This is the subject of Part Two. But research and analysis are not enough, either, no matter how well they are done. Certain intellectuals have been criticized for doing only analysis, for saying what needs to be done but not how to do it. We feel these criticisms are justified. In Part Three, therefore, we deal with mobilization.

Finally, since community organizing involves interacting with flesh-and-blood human beings, it is essential to know how to facilitate a group and to foster internal democracy in order to ensure that collective action is as effective as possible. Our aim here is not to provide techniques of manipulation, as is sometimes the case, but rather to offer methods of promoting group consciousness. We also felt it essential to deal with the problems of funding and the possible dissolution of a group.

Community organizing, however, is not merely a matter of technique. It is above all a social process involving the whole personality of the organizer. For this reason, we have throughout the book emphasized attitudes as well as skills. We should add that there can be no one model for community organizers, and that success or failure does not depend on the organizer's personality or even on his or her political correctness. To believe the contrary is to fall into a kind of simplistic voluntarism, a belief that wanting to do something is enough to be able to do it, a notion that is akin to the dominant ideology's tendency to blame the victim. This bring us, in the last part of the book, to attempt to situate the ideologies and concrete practices of community organizing today in the broader socio-political context.

New Fields, New Practices, New Terms

For many, the Eighties have been a time to reconsider community action as a viable option. The critical political and economic situation of the early decade has led to a wave of conservatism that has had considerable effect on community organizing. The rules have changed, and the old players are being pushed off the field by younger ones with a different cultural background, who have understood the need to develop a new style of organizing. Oppression and injustice are still with us — if anything, they are stronger — but the new political context forces us to take a new look at needs and means. More than twenty years ago Bob Dylan said, "The times, they are a-changin'…" and "You don't need a weatherman to know which way the wind blows." Today, in North America, the wind is not blowing to the left!

In Canada, federal, provincial, and, with a few exceptions, local governments are pursuing policies set by Margaret Thatcher. The endorsement of continentalism in the Free Trade Agreement between Canada and the U.S. will only increase pressure to "harmonize"

Canadian social programmes — downward. The poor get poorer, the old get older, and the social needs of our industrialized society grow greater while government leaders try to trim the welfare state.

New fields

The heightened political awareness of the Seventies stimulated the growth of a range of community groups and voluntary organizations that are distinct from the more class-based popular groups. The proletariat has been replaced by low-income families, abused women, the physically and mentally handicapped, and unemployed youth as a base for organizing.

There are men's groups, women's shelters, organizations for people with all sorts of handicaps, parents of the handicapped, elderly people and pensioners, caregivers, and environmental, peace, and literacy groups. New groups have formed and organized actions in old and new areas of activity. Socio-economic issues have broadened to include economic development and cultural and recreational questions. The popular movement, once centred on the plight of the poor, welfare recipients, the unemployed, tenants, and non-unionized minimum-wage workers, has broadened its population base and its activities.

New practices

This new blood has brought new perspectives and a new style. One major difference is a more pragmatic approach to issues. Ideological debates have been replaced by discussion on practical, technical, and organizational issues. Winnable bread-and-butter issues are the order of the day. People must have a good handle on issues in order to get involved... which has always been a good organizing principle. Concrete issues are still rooted in the democratic ethic of the Sixties and Seventies. Women's centres are a good example. They sprang up in the Eighties as a direct result of the ideological battle for equal rights. Today, their work is less elitist, much more involved with everyday concerns such as daycare and job training programmes for women.

They have a much broader base, going beyond the "liberated" middle classes that were over-represented in the women's movement.

This pragmatism has also meant a new approach to funding, particularly with regard to money from business and the State. "Class enemies" have become necessary evils, and even partners. It is not unusual to see a local business sponsor a women's shelter or a youth centre. The recent creation of Community Economic Development Corporations in communities such as Pointe St-Charles and Victoriaville after failed attempts in the Sixties and early Seventies has encouraged community groups to look to the traditional business community for support. The trend is toward broad coalitions on very concrete issues in the areas of the environment and housing. The building of low-cost housing on the site of the former CPR Angus Shops in the Rosemont district of Montréal was the result of one such initiative. The style of relations with funding organizations has changed and political virginity is a thing of the past.

The approach to coalition-building has also been influenced by this pragmatism. Coalitions now tend to be short-term, involving concrete issues and minimal structure. This is the age of the disposable coalition. The top-heavy centralizing bureaucratic organizations of the past have given way to a certain localism and parochialism. When groups join together they want results. There is almost a cost-benefit approach to the decision to join a coalition. Dogmatism is dead, and groups are more open to exchanging services and promoting common concerns. Coalitions are more numerous but more short-lived.

There is acceptance of marketing and lobbying by community organizations, although some nostalgic organizers are still reluctant to accept them. In a context of large numbers of groups and diverse interests, and few Québec-wide organizations, everyone thinks first of one's own survival. This is the corollary of pragmatism.

Finally, there is the professionalization of staff in community groups. The twenty-four-hour-a-day, young, healthy, unattached, workaholic activist with a cause has been replaced by the unionized professional concerned about burn-out and the protection of privacy and family life. Today's honest, hard-working — and probably more well-balanced — employees are looking for recognition and improved working conditions: working conditions that, in any case, will always be far from equal to those of public-sector employees.

New terms

Citizens' groups became "popular groups" in the Seventies and "community groups" in the Eighties. As we approach the Nineties, they are fast becoming "voluntary action groups." These terms reflect the politics of the national, municipal, and neighbourhood arenas. When the welfare state became a major source of funding, groups had to define their positions accordingly. Today, as neo-conservative governments call into question the role of the State, groups are defining themselves as voluntary, meaning "non-State" and free to act independently.

As politics have evolved, the terminology has evolved. The "global approach" of the Seventies has given way to the "community approach" of the recent Rochon Commission. Everything has become "community" in the Eighties, from services to businesses and shops. It is the "in" word that goes with the small-is-beautiful, quality-of-life, decentralized, localist, individual-responsibility approach, and this falls in line with the State's opting out of social programmes or coopting voluntary initiatives to take responsibility for them. The Québec ministry of health and social services confuses and manipulates people into believing that public or profit-making services are "community" (for and by the community) while decision-making remains highly centralized. The State has given a bureaucratic, technocratic sense to the word "community" by narrowing its meaning to target populations, priorities, and programmes that are imposed on public institutions, such as CLSCs and voluntary action groups.

The case of the "community approach" exemplifies this confusion. This approach, which many CLSCs have decided to adopt, involves the use of community resources to solve individual social and health problems (social casework) and a group work approach. It also includes a community organizing approach based on the ideas of Murray Ross, which involves creating resources in the community to "service" people. The "community approach" definitely does not mean community action for change, or challenging existing institutions. Caution is required when reading or using the word "community" in relation to any dealings with the State.

Issues, Debates, and Challenges

A number of issues facing community organization as a field, and community groups as actors in society, are currently being debated among community groups in Québec. They could lead to new challenges for organizers and groups.

Issues

Times are both difficult and good for community organizations. There is less broad-based mobilization, but community groups and community work in general, including services to individuals, are now recognized as a viable alternative to the State monopoly on social services. But we are still in a context of neo-conservative ideology in which the emphasis is on the self, individual responsibility, privacy, and entrepreneurship. The "pull-yourself-up-by-the-bootstraps" ethic of the "Iron Lady" has replaced the individualist revolt expressed by heavy metal rock groups like "Iron Maiden." Meanwhile, the collective revolution of the music of the Sixties is coming back, but only as nostalgia. If we become fixed nostalgically on the massive demonstrations of the past, we are in danger of losing sight of the present and failing to prepare for the future.

That future is already upon us in the form of a programmed, controlled society — all in the name of freedom of the individual. Welfare reform means workfare programmes in many provinces and States. Deinstitutionalization and privatization of public health and social services are on the agenda of most governments. These policies create tremendous stress for individuals, families, and community service groups by dumping the elderly, the handicapped, and the unemployed in their laps, all in the name of less government, more individual freedom, and more community involvement.

The union movement is also losing strength. Membership is down, and big private and public enterprises are sub-contracting more and more to small, low-paying, non-unionized firms. Unions often make concessions in hopes of saving their members' jobs. A major ally of community groups and progressive movements is losing ground.

Finally, the welfare state is being called into question and welfare pluralism proposed as an alternative to State monopoly. The criticism comes from the left as much as from the right. Community groups are mushrooming to meet new needs and are providing direct services to individuals, often offering a quality alternative to State services at a lower cost. However, the burden of providing services and the heavy bureaucratic requirements related to funding limit their freedom to carry out community action aimed at institutional change. Their very existence is in constant jeopardy because of their dependence on public funding, even though they have been recognized in policy papers as essential partners in the field of social services in a pluralistic democratic society. New strategies and tactics must be found if community organizing is to survive in the current context without caving in.

Current debates

Should community organizing take a soft line, take risks, go on the offensive, or seek to create innovative alternatives with backing by business and the State? Should it be more cautious and defensive, making the traditional demands, protecting acquired rights, and calling for justice? These are the issues currently being debated. There are still many basic questions to be resolved, and unrecognized rights to be fought for.

Is it possible to cooperate with State institutions in community struggles on such issues as transportation, the environment, economic development, and peace? Should community groups and federations come together in broad national or provincial organizations, forums, or coalitions to stop the dismantling of the welfare state? Such coalitions have been short-lived in Québec, even with (or because of) strong support and financial involvement from the unions. Popular Solidarity Québec has existed since 1986 and is the most broadly based coalition working to protect the welfare state from neo-conservative governments, but it has still not involved all sectors and its impact has not been great.

Challenges

The future of community organizing as a profession and of community organizations, or voluntary action groups, depends to a great extent on whether they are able to roll with the punches. More emphasis will have to be put on marketing images, and gaining recognition and funding, but this must not occur at any cost. Organizations that have come together democratically to bring about social and political change through collective action while respecting the individuality of their members have a unique quality that is essential in our society. The challenge is to adapt to changing times, and to combine tactical compromises and long-term goals of structural change. This also means making more room for individual development within collective goals.

Similarly, groups should consider accepting the offer of partnership by the Québec provincial government —but with conditions. As the State develops its social policies, it must recognize and respect the nature of community groups, supporting them but not controlling them to the point of destroying their distinct qualities. As in a federal constitution or a free-trade agreement, respect for the partner's autonomy is essential. The challenge for community organizations is to gain recognition and funding while maintaining a critical perspective on society and challenging State policies with strong grass-roots membership and support.

NAMES OF ORGANIZATIONS

ACEFs (Associations coopératives d'économie familiale) — Cooperative Family Budget Associations.

ADDS (Association pour la défense des droits sociaux) — Association for the Defense of Social Rights.

Adult Education Service — Service d'éducation des adultes.

AFEAS (Associations féminines d'Education et d'Action sociale) — Women's Education and Social Action Associations.

Amitié service troisième age (ASTA) — Seniors' Friendship and Service — in the Montréal working-class neighbourhood of Hochelaga-Maisonneuve. In the area of home care for the aged, the two organizations of ASTA and Place Vermeil, in south-central Montréal, are more progressive than any government programme.

AQDR (Association québécoise pour la défense des droits des retraité-e-s et pré-retraité-e-s) — Québec Association for the Rights of the Retired.

Association for the Defense of Social Rights — Association pour la défense des droits sociaux (ADDS).

Association pour la défense des droits sociaux (ADDS) — Association for the Defense of Social Rights.

Association québécoise pour la défense des droits des retraité-e-s et pré-retraité-e-s (AQDR) — Québec Association for the Rights of the Retired — an organization of people fifty-five years of age and older set up in the Eighties and ideologically similar to the Grey Power movement; counts dozens of local groups, and with the population aging rapidly could become a most significant pressure group in the Nineties.

Associations coopératives d'économie familiale (ACEFs) — Cooperative Family Budget Associations — born in the mid-Sixties as an extension of the work of the Confédération des syndicats nationaux (CSN — Confederation of National Trade Unions) into the area of consumerism; based on the work of Ralph Nader, they have since developed their own approaches.

Associations féminines d'Education et d'Action sociale (AFEAS) — Women's Education and Social Action Associations — a longstanding organization with six hundred active groups in Québec. Once identified with Catholic orthodoxy and political conservatism, the AFEAS groups now play an increasingly important role in campaigns for recognition of the economic value of housework, inclusion of women in the Québec Pension Plan, and wages for housewives.

ASTA (Amitié service troisième age) — Seniors' Friendship and Service.

Au Bas de l'Echelle — Rank and File.

Autonomous Women's Movement — Mouvement autonome des femmes.

Autonomous Youth Organization — Regroupement Autonome des Jeunes (RAJ).

BAEQ (Bureau d'aménagement de l'est du Québec) — Eastern Québec Planning and Development Office.

Big March for Jobs — Grande marche pour l'emploi.

Bois-Francs Community Development Corporation — Corporation du Développement communautaire des Bois-Francs.

Bureau d'aménagement de l'est du Québec (BAEQ) — Eastern Québec Planning and Development Office — involved a large-scale social animation programme, in the Sixties, with the population of the Gaspé Peninsula and the Lower St. Lawrence region. When people realized that this was intended to manipulate them rather than to involve them in planning and development for their region, they banded together in Opération dignité groups and succeeded to a large extent in blocking the plans of the State.

Bureaux d'aide juridique — Legal Aid Offices.

Caisse populaire — parish credit union.

Canadian Association for Adult Education — Institut canadien d'Education des Adultes (ICEA).

Centraide — Québec equivalent of United Way.

Centre de formation populaire — Popular Training Centre.

Centre des Femmes des Cantons — Eastern Townships Women's Centre.

Centre populaire de documentation —Popular Resource Centre.

Centres d'éducation populaire — Popular Education Centres.

Centres de santé des femmes — Women's Health Centres.

Centres de services sociaux (CSS) — Social Service Centres. There are fourteen Social Service Centres that, together, cover all of Québec. Whereas the 162 CLSCs offer front-line services, Social Service Centres provide more specialized services. They are also responsible for child protection.

Centres locaux de services communautaires (CLSC) — Local Community Service Centres — neighbourhood health and social service institutions under the ministry of health and social services.

Cercle d'économie de la future ménagère — Future Brides' Hope Chest.

CLSC (Centres locaux de services communautaires) — Local Community Service Centres.

Coalition for a Rent Freeze — Regroupement pour le gel des loyers.

Comité des îlots St-Martin — St. Martin Blocks Committee.

Common Front of Welfare Recipients of Québec — Front commun des assistées sociales et assistés sociaux du Québec.

Conseil de développement social — Council on Social Development (formerly Conseil des oeuvres — Council of Charities).

Conseil des oeuvres — Council of Charities (former name of Conseil de développement social — Council on Social Development).

Conseil du statut de la femme — Québec Council on the Status of Women.

Consumer Protection Office — Office de protection du consommateur.

Coopérative d'action communautaire des citoyens de Hochelaga-Maisonneuve — Hochelaga-Maisonneuve Citizens' Community Action Cooperative.

Cooperative Family Budget Associations — Associations coopératives d'économie familiale (ACEFs).

Corporation du Développement communautaire des Bois-Francs — Bois-Francs Community Development Corporation.

Council of Charities — Conseil des oeuvres (former name of Council on Social Development — Conseil de développement social).

Council on Social Development — Conseil de développement social (formerly Council of Charities — Conseil des oeuvres).

CSS (Centres de services sociaux) — Social Service Centres.

Disabled Persons Bureau — Office des personnes handicapées.

Eastern Townships Women's Centre — Centre des Femmes des Cantons.

Family Budget Service — Service d'économie familiale.

FCABQ (Fédération des Centres d'Action bénévole du Québec) — Québec Federation of Volunteer Centres.

Fédération des Centres d'Action bénévole du Québec (FCABQ) — Québec Federation of Volunteer Centres — in existence for some twelve years, it includes some fifty Centres d'action bénévole locaux — Local Volunteer Centres.

Federation of Community Daycare Centres — Regroupement des garderies populaires.

Federation of Women's Centres — Regroupement des Centres de Femmes.

Federation of Women's Shelters — Regroupement des Maisons d'Hébergement.

FRAP (Front d'action politique) — Political Action Front.

FRAPRU (Front d'action populaire et de réaménagement urbain) — Front for Popular Action on Urban Planning.

Front commun des assistées sociales et assistés sociaux du Québec — Common Front of Welfare Recipients of Québec.

Front d'action politique (FRAP) — Political Action Front — included people involved both in popular groups and unions. Organized by social animators, FRAP never recovered from the repression it suffered during the October Crisis.

Front d'action populaire et de réaménagement urbain (FRAPRU) — Front for Popular Action on Urban Planning — a provincial organization that carries out research and action to promote the interests of working-class people in the area of housing and urban planning.

Front de libération des femmes — Women's Liberation Front.

Front for Popular Action on Urban Planning — Front d'action populaire et de réaménagement urbain (FRAPRU).

Future Brides' Hope Chest — Cercle d'économie de la future ménagère.

Grande marche pour l'emploi — Big March for Jobs.

Hochelaga-Maisonneuve Citizens' Community Action Cooperative — Coopérative d'action communautaire des citoyens de Hochelaga-Maisonneuve.

Human Rights and Liberties League — Ligue des Droits et Libertés.

ICEA (Institut canadien d'Education des Adultes) — Canadian Association for Adult Education.

Institut canadien d'Education des Adultes (ICEA) — Canadian Association for Adult Education — the autonomous Québec counterpart of the Canadian organization of the same name.

Legal Aid Offices — Bureaux d'aide juridique.

Ligue des Droits et Libertés — Human Rights and Liberties League.

Local Community Service Centres — Centres locaux de services communautaires (CLSC).

Maison des chômeurs de Saint-Henri — Saint Henri Neighbourhood Unemployed House.

Mouvement Action-Chômage — Unemployment Action Movement.

Mouvement autonome des femmes — Autonomous Women's Movement.

Mouvement socialiste — Socialist Movement. (Translators' note: A political movement formed in the early Eighties whose programme includes socialism, feminism, and independence for Québec.)

Office de protection du consommateur — Consumer Protection Bureau.

Office des personnes handicapées — Disabled Persons Bureau.

Opération dignité — groups formed when people realized that the Sixties large-scale social animation programme among the population of the Gaspé Peninsula and the Lower St. Lawrence region, planned by the Bureau d'aménagement de l'est du Québec (BAEQ)— Eastern Québec Planning and Development Office — was intended to manipulate them rather than to involve them in planning and development for their region. They succeeded to a large extent in blocking the plans of the State. The spirit of Opération dignité is still in evidence today in the struggle against the closing of rural post offices.

People's Organizing and Information Project — Projet d'organisation populaire, d'information et de regroupement (POPIR).

PEP (Programme économique de Pointe St-Charles) — Pointe St. Charles Economic Programme.

Place Vermeil — a seniors' group in south-central Montréal, which, with Amitié service troisième age (ASTA) — Seniors' Friendship and Service, is more progressive than any government programme regarding policy of home care for the aged.

Pointe St. Charles Economic Programme — Programme économique de Pointe St-Charles (PEP).

Political Action Front — Front d'action politique (FRAP).

POPIR (Projet d'organisation populaire, d'information et de regroupement) — People's Organizing and Information Project.

Popular Education Centres — Centres d'éducation populaire.

Popular Resource Centre — Centre populaire de documentation.

Popular Summits — Sommets populaires.

Popular Training Centre — Centre de formation populaire.

Popular Urban Planning Service — Service d'aménagement populaire.

Programme économique de Pointe St-Charles (PEP) — Pointe St. Charles Economic Programme.

Projet d'organisation populaire, d'information et de regroupement (POPIR)— People's Organizing and Information Project. (Translators' note: POPIR is a homonym for *pas pire*, meaning "not bad," a standard response in colloquial Québec French when someone asks how you are.)

Québec Association for the Rights of the Retired — Association québécoise pour la défense des droits des retraité-e-s et pré-retraité-e-s (AQDR).

Québec Council on the Status of Women — Conseil du statut de la femme.

Québec Farmers' Union — Union des producteurs agricoles.

Québec Federation of Volunteer Centres — Fédération des Centres d'Action bénévole du Québec (FCABQ).

Québec Rental Board — Régie du logement.

Québec Popular Solidarity — Solidarité populaire Québec.

RAJ (Regroupement Autonome des Jeunes) — Autonomous Youth Organization.

Rank and File — Au Bas de l'Echelle.

Régie du logement — Québec Rental Board.

Regroupement Autonome des Jeunes (RAJ) — Autonomous Youth Coalition — an organization of students and young workers that denounces the living conditions imposed on persons under the age of thirty, particularly the discrimination against this age group in determining welfare benefits. (Translators' note:

Under-thirties receive basic welfare benefits of $178 per month, compared to the $487 minimum given to a person over thirty. In French, *RAJ* is a homonym for "rage.")

Regroupement des Centres de Femmes — Federation of Women's Centres. Founded in 1984, it currently brings together seventy-five centres involved in information, education, and social action for women.

Regroupement des garderies populaires — Federation of Community Daycare Centres.

Regroupement des Maisons d'Hébergement — Federation of Women's Shelters — an association of shelters for battered women made up of about fifty groups funded primarily by the State, which has officially recognized the need for such services.

Regroupement pour le gel des loyers — Coalition for a Rent Freeze.

Saint Henri Neighbourhood Unemployed House — Maison des chômeurs de Saint-Henri.

Seniors' Friendship and Service — Amitié service troisième age (ASTA).

Service d'aménagement populaire — Popular Urban Planning Service.

Service d'économie familiale — Family Budget Service.

Service d'éducation des adultes — Adult Education Service.

Socialist Movement — Mouvement socialiste.

Social Service Centres — Centres de services sociaux (CSS).

Solidarité populaire Québec — Québec Popular Solidarity.

Sommets populaires — Popular Summits — a popular response to the Parti québécois government's creation of summits bringing together interest groups on a series of broad issues. Popular Summits have also been held as protests against the economic summits of the seven rich industrialized nations, most recently in Toronto in June 1988.

St. Martin Blocks Committee — Comité des îlots St-Martin.

Travailleurs-étudiants du Québec — Worker-Students of Québec.

Unemployment Action Movement — Mouvement Action-Chômage.

Union des producteurs agricoles — Québec Farmers' Union.

Women's Education and Social Action Associations — Associations féminines d'Education et d'Action sociale (AFEAS).

Women's Health Centres — Centres de santé des femmes.

Women's Liberation Front — Front de libération des femmes.

Worker-Students of Québec — Travailleurs-étudiants du Québec.

BIBLIOGRAPHY

Alinsky, Saul. *Rules for Radicals* (New York: Random House, 1971).

Artaud, Marcel. "Le financement des groupes populaires. Le commerce des idées doit-il être déficitaire?" in *Le Temps fou*, No. 12 (Dec. 1980).

Baccouche, N. "L'intervention de l'intellectuel dans le social" in *Revue canadienne d'éducation en service social*, Vol. 5, No. 1 (1979).

Beaudry, Lucille. *Guide de recherche à l'intention des militants* (Montréal: Centre coopératif de recherches en politique sociale, 1975).

Blondin, Michel. "L'animation sociale en milieu urbain: une solution" in *Recherches sociographiques*, Vol. 6, No. 3 (1965).

Bourdieu, Pierre, Jean-Claude Chamboredon, and Jean-Claude Passeron. *Le Métier de sociologue* (Paris: Mouton/Bordas, 1968).

Brecht, Bertolt. "The Exception and the Rule" in *The Jewish Wife and Other Short Plays*, trans. Eric Bentley (New York: Grove Press, 1965).

Chamboredon, Jean-Claude. "La délinquance juvénile, essai de construction d'objet" in *Revue française de sociologie*, Vol. 12, (1971).

Couillard, Robert, and Robert Mayer. "La pratique d'organisation communautaire à la maison de quartier de Pointe St-Charles" in *Revue internationale d'action communautaire*, No. 4/44 (1980).

De Bousquet, Marie-Hélène. *Le Service social* (Paris: Presses Universitaires de France, collection Que sais-je, No. 1173, 1965).

De Cock, B., and J. Grané. "Travail social et classes sociales" in J.P. Liégois, ed., *Idéologie et Pratique du travail social de prévention* (Toulouse: Privat, 1977).

De Robertis, C., and H. Pascal. *L'Intervention collective en travail social* (Paris: Le Centurion, 1987).

Deslauriers, Jean-Pierre. "Guide de recherche qualitative" in *Bulletin de recherche*, No. 62 (1982).

Desroches, Henri. *Apprentissage en sciences sociales et éducation permanente* (Paris: Editions Ouvrières, 1971).

Duchastel, J. *Marcel Rioux: Entre l'utopie et la raison* (Montréal: Nouvelle optique, 1981).

Guay, Jérôme. *L'Intervenant professionnel face à l'aide naturelle* (Chicoutimi, Qué.: G. Morin Editeur, 1984).

Jacob, André. *Guide méthodologique pour la recherche et l'action sociale* (Montréal: Nouvelles Frontières, 1984).

Kayser, Bernard. "Sans enquête, pas de droit de parole" in *Hérodote*, No. 9 (1978).

Lamarche, François. *Une Ville à vendre (Cahier 1: Pour une analyse marxiste de la question urbaine)* (Québec: Conseil des Oeuvres de Québec, 1972).

Lesemann, Frédéric. "Stratégies d'intervention auprès des individus et des collectivités: l'action communautaire" in *Les Cahiers de santé communautaire*, No. 2 (1979).

Malavoy, M., and N. St-Martin. "La formation pratique, ou apprendre dans l'action" in *Les Cahiers de recherche en travail social*, No. 23 (1982).

Marquart, Françoise. "La recherche peut-elle être social" in *Informations sociales*, No. 7 (July 1973).

Médard, Jean. *Communauté locale et Organisation communautaire aux Etats-Unis* (Paris: A. Colin, 1969).

Nison, André. "Propositions méthodologiques" in *Travail social et Méthodes d'enquête sociologique* (Paris: Les Editions ESF, 1975).

O'Neil, Michel. "Santé communautaire et communauté: de l'influence de deux conceptions de la communauté sur les interventions québécoises en éducation sanitaire" in *Les Cahiers de santé communautaire*, No. 2 (1979).

Ouellet-Dubé, Francine. "Recherche ou pratique: qui gagne?" in *Service social*, Vol. 28, No. 2-3 (1979).

Paiement, Guy. "Comment ça marche, l'analyse sociale?" in *Relations* (Dec. 1982).

Poulin, Martin. "L'étude monographique des communautés" in *Service social*, Vol. 27, No. 1 (Jan.-June 1978).

Rhéaume, Jacques. "La recherche-action: un nouveau mode de savoir?" *Sociologie et Sociétés*, Vol. 14, No. 1 (1982).

Séguier, Michel. *Critique institutionnelle et Créativité collective* (Paris: Editions L'Harmattan, 1976).

Sellier, F. "Le rôle des organisations et des institutions dans le développement des besoins sociaux" in *Sociologie du travail*, Vol. 12, No. 1 (Jan.-March 1970).

Warren, Roland L. *Studying Your Community*, 3rd ed. (New York: Free Press, 1969).

THE POLITICS OF HUMAN SERVICES
by Steven Wineman

A scathing personal and political account of Wineman's experience as a welfare worker, offering a concrete, detailed plan for wholesale conversion of existing human services programmes. His strategy for "radical decentralisation" combines the struggles of oppressed and marginalized groups in an integrated movement for change. He envisions businesses, housing, health care and support networks that are democratically run, co-operatively managed and controlled by the people who use them.

Wineman makes a stong case against capitalism and the welfare state.
Books in Canada

272 pages
Paperback ISBN: 0-920057-43-8 $14.95
Hardcover ISBN: 0-920057-42-X $29.95

THE SEARCH FOR COMMUNITY
From Utopia to a Co-operative Society
by George Melnyk

Co-ops in different countries are assessed for strengths and drawbacks as he selects the components that can be adapted to our society and used to link groups already functioning. The result is the "social co-operative," a new citizen-run structure that will successfully respond to our social and economic requirements.

Melnyk offers a fascinating social history of co-operatives, from monastery to commune.
Choice

170 pages
Paperback ISBN: 0-920057-52-7 $14.95
Hardcover ISBN: 0-920057-53-5 $34.95

SERVICES AND CIRCUSES
Community and the Welfare State
by Frédéric Lesemann
translated by Lorne Huston and Margaret Heap

The Quiet Revolution turned Québec's entire health and welfare system on its head. Suddenly, an immense government bureaucracy took over the services traditionally administered by the Church and local voluntary societies.

This analysis points out the dangers of stripping local groups of their power, and raises important questions about who really benefits from state welfarism. Although the author focuses on the rapid shift from clerical to government control during the 1960s in Québec, *Services and Circuses* is relevant for all Canadians as the various levels of government and their technocrats become even more powerful.

277 pages
Paperback ISBN: 0-920057-05-5 $12.95
Hardcover ISBN: 0-920057-06-3 $29.95

WORK AND MADNESS
The Rise of Community Psychiatry
by Diana Ralph

A social worker, teacher and community activist, Diana Ralph takes on contemporary community mental health systems. In a meticulously researched and highly readable work, the growth and change in the definition and treatment of mental health disorders is subjected to a concerned and scholarly scrutiny.

Ralph finds available theories, from the liberal to the Marxist to the radical antipsychiatry approaches, inadequate in accounting for these changes. Instead, she locates the ideological origins of community psychiatry within the tradition of industrial psychology, and is able to show how its operation is linked to the needs of contemporary industrial management in their efforts to defuse dissatisfaction and alienation in the workplace.

Concise, well-written, thoroughly researched, with excellent primary and secondary sources.
Choice

206 pages, bibliography
Paperback ISBN: 0-919619-04-5 $9.95
Hardcover ISBN: 0-919619-07-X $29.95

BLACK ROSE BOOKS

has published the following books of related interests

Peter Kropotkin, Memoirs of a Revolutionist, introduction by George Woodcock
Peter Kropotkin, Mutual Aid, introduction by George Woodcock
Peter Kropotkin, The Great French Revolution, introduction by George Woodcock
Peter Kropotkin, The Conquest of Bread, introduction by George Woodcock
     other books by Peter Kropotkin are forthcoming in this series
Marie Fleming, The Geography of Freedom: The Odyssey of Elisée Reclus,
     introduction by George Woodcock
William R. McKercher, Freedom and Authority
Noam Chomksy, Language and Poltics, edited by C.P. Otero
Noam Chomsky, Radical Priorities, edited by C.P. Otero
George Woodcock, Pierre-Joseph Proudhon: A Biography
Murray Bookchin, Remaking Society
Murray Bookchin, Toward an Ecological Society
Murray Bookchin, Post-Scarcity Anarchism
Murray Bookchin, The Limits of the City
Murray Bookchin, The Modern Crisis
Edith Thomas, Louise Michel: A Biography
Walter Johnson, Trade Unions and the State
John Clark, The Anarchist Moment: Reflections on Culture, Nature and Power
Sam Dolgoff, Bakunin on Anarchism
Sam Dolgoff, The Anarchist Collectives
Sam Dolgoff, The Cuban Revolution: A Critical Perspective
Thom Holterman, Law and Anarchism
Stephen Schecter, The Politics of Urban Liberation
Etienne de la Boétie, The Politics of Obedience
Abel Paz, Durruti, the people armed
Juan Gomez Casas, Anarchist Organisation: The History of the F.A.I.
Voline, The Unknown Revolution
Dimitrios Roussopoulos, The Anarchist Papers
Dimitrios Roussopoulos, The Anarchist Papers 2

send for a complete catalogue of books
mailed out free
BLACK ROSE BOOKS
3981 boul. St-Laurent #444
Montréal, Québec H2W 1Y5 Canada

Printed by the workers of
Editions Marquis, Montmagny, Québec, Canada
for
Black Rose Books Ltd.